Upper-intermediate

GLOBAL GATE

— Video-based Four Skills Training —

Hironobu Tanaka　　Mika Igarashi　　Bill Benfield　　Akira Morita

SEIBIDO

photographs by

iStockphoto / Shutterstock / Getty Images

株式会社Ashirase / AFP＝時事 / GRANGER/時事通信フォト

videos by

Ready to Run

StreamLine

Web 動画・音声ファイルのストリーミング再生について

CD マーク及び Web 動画マークがある箇所は、PC、スマートフォン、タブレット端末において、無料でストリーミング再生することができます。下記 URL よりご利用ください。再生手順や動作環境などは本書巻末の「Web 動画のご案内」をご覧ください。

https://st.seibido.co.jp

音声ファイルのダウンロードについて

CD マークがある箇所は、ダウンロードすることも可能です。下記 URL の書籍詳細ページにあるダウンロードアイコンをクリックしてください。

https://www.seibido.co.jp/ad687

CONTENTS

LEARNING OVERVIEW

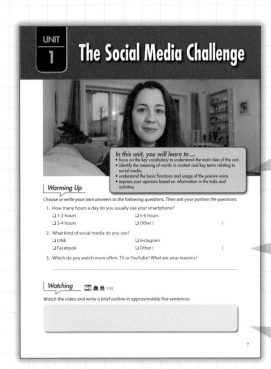

In this unit, you will learn to ...

An overview of the unit helps students focus on learning outcomes.

Warming Up

Activates students' background knowledge of the topic.

Watching

Presents a video for students to watch and then outline in a few sentences.

Vocabulary

Teaches collocations, idioms, and useful expressions from the video.

Tips on Listening and Speaking

Presents useful information for listening and speaking.

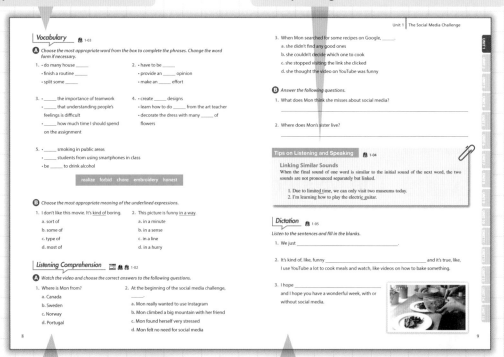

Listening Comprehension

Presents various review questions for students to check comprehension.

Dictation

Teaches sound features related to Tips on Listening and Speaking as well as content words from the video.

Retelling

Presents parts of the video for students to watch and retell in their own words.

Grammar

Presents a thorough explanation of the grammar point of the unit.

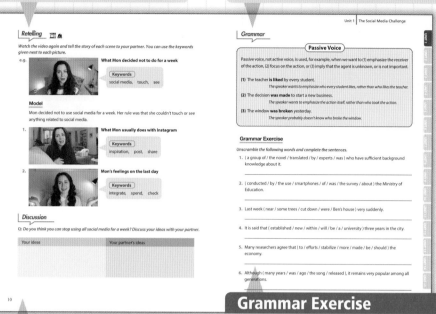

Discussion

Presents a topic-related question to enhance students' critical thinking skills.

Grammar Exercise

Enhances students' grammar ability through a word-order exercise.

Vocabulary Check

Teaches useful vocabulary from the Reading.

Reading

Features an interesting article related to the topic of the video.

Reading Comprehension

Presents open-ended questions for students to check comprehension.

LEARNING OVERVIEW

Writing

A *Write about your thoughts on sharing aspects of your personal life on social media in 70-80 words, considering the following points.*

❑ Do you think it is a good idea to share aspects of your personal life on social media?
❑ What are the pros of sharing aspects of your personal life on social media?
❑ What are the cons of sharing aspects of your personal life on social media?

Useful Expressions

I believe that sharing aspects of my personal life on social media is …
One of the advantages/disadvantages of sharing aspects of my personal life on social media is …
Sharing my pictures with others may be nice because …
Sharing what I'm thinking may be important because …
It is sometimes dangerous for us to share …

Useful Vocabulary

interact with followers   check reactions of other people   receive comments from friends
post some photos from my trip   be concerned about privacy

B *Make pairs and share your ideas with your partner. Write down what your partner has shared with you.*

14

> **Writing**
> Presents useful points to organize students' ideas or opinions and boost their writing abilities.

> **Useful Expressions for Discussions**
> Presents useful expressions for each discussion exercise.

Useful Expressions for Discussions

Reacting

☐ I see your point.
☐ I find that quite interesting [amazing / outstanding / intriguing].
☐ That's a good [great / key / fundamental] idea.
☐ Really? I didn't know [wasn't aware of] that.
☐ Could you please elaborate?
☐ I'm intrigued. Tell me more.

Giving your opinion

☐ In my opinion [In my view / From my perspective], …
☐ I think [believe / feel / suppose] …
☐ My opinion [idea / stance / belief] is that …
☐ I'd like to say [express] that …
☐ As far as I can see, …

Giving yourself time to think

☐ Let me take a moment to think.
☐ That's an interesting question that requires some thought.
☐ I've never considered that before.

Asking for clarification

☐ Could you kindly repeat that?
☐ Would you mind speaking a bit slower?
☐ Could you rephrase that, please?
☐ Can you simplify your explanation?
☐ Could you clarify what you meant by …

Agreeing

☐ I totally [entirely / completely / strongly] agree with you.
☐ I agree with your idea [opinion / thought / suggestion / proposal].
☐ I'm in complete agreement.
☐ I see no objections to that.
☐ That certainly makes sense to me.
☐ I'm with you on this.

Disagreeing politely

☐ I appreciate your point, but I think …
☐ I understand your perspective, but in my view, …
☐ It's an interesting viewpoint, but I have a different perspective.
☐ While that may be true, I would argue that …

Showing importance

☐ A is important [crucial / significant / essential], because …
☐ One crucial factor to consider is …
☐ The key focus here is …
☐ We must prioritize [put priority on] … because …

Focusing on one topic

☐ On this particular issue [matter / topic / aspect / case / point], …
☐ When it comes to this specific point, …
☐ Regarding this matter, …

128   129

UNIT 1

The Social Media Challenge

In this unit, you will learn to ...
- focus on the key vocabulary to understand the main idea of the unit.
- identify the meaning of words in context and key terms relating to social media.
- understand the basic functions and usage of the passive voice.
- express your opinions based on information in the tasks and activities.

Warming Up

Choose or write your own answers to the following questions. Then ask your partner the questions.

1. How many hours a day do you usually use your smartphone?
   - ❏ 1-2 hours   ❏ 5-6 hours
   - ❏ 3-4 hours   ❏ Other (   )

2. What kind of social media do you use?
   - ❏ LINE   ❏ Instagram
   - ❏ Facebook   ❏ Other (   )

3. Which do you watch more often, TV or YouTube? What are your reasons?

   _____

Watching

WEB動画 🖥️ 📀 DVD 📀 CD 1-02

Watch the video and write a brief outline in approximately five sentences.

Vocabulary 🎧 1-03

A *Choose the most appropriate word from the box to complete the phrases. Change the word form if necessary.*

1. • do many house _____
   • finish a routine _____
   • split some _____

2. • have to be _____
   • provide an _____ opinion
   • make an _____ effort

3. • _____ the importance of teamwork
   • _____ that understanding people's feelings is difficult
   • _____ how much time I should spend on the assignment

4. • create _____ designs
   • learn how to do _____ from the art teacher
   • decorate the dress with many _____ of flowers

5. • _____ smoking in public areas
   • _____ students from using smartphones in class
   • be _____ to drink alcohol

| realize   forbid   chore   embroidery   honest |

B *Choose the most appropriate meaning of the underlined expressions.*

1. I don't like this movie. It's <u>kind of</u> boring.
   a. sort of
   b. some of
   c. type of
   d. most of

2. This picture is funny <u>in a way</u>.
   a. in a minute
   b. in a sense
   c. in a line
   d. in a hurry

Listening Comprehension WEB動画 💻 📀 DVD 🎧 CD 1-02

A *Watch the video and choose the correct answers to the following questions.*

1. Where is Mon from?
   a. Canada
   b. Sweden
   c. Norway
   d. Portugal

2. At the beginning of the social media challenge, _____.
   a. Mon really wanted to use Instagram
   b. Mon climbed a big mountain with her friend
   c. Mon found herself very stressed
   d. Mon felt no need for social media

3. When Mon searched for some recipes on Google, _____.

    a. she didn't find any good ones

    b. she couldn't decide which one to cook

    c. she stopped visiting the link she clicked

    d. she thought the video on YouTube was funny

B *Answer the following questions.*

1. What does Mon think she misses about social media?

_____

2. Where does Mon's sister live?

_____

Tips on Listening and Speaking 1-04

Linking Similar Sounds
When the final sound of one word is similar to the initial sound of the next word, the two sounds are not pronounced separately but linked.

    1. Due to limited time, we can only visit two museums today.
    2. I'm learning how to play the electric guitar.

Dictation 1-05

Listen to the sentences and fill in the blanks.

1. We just _____.

2. It's kind of, like, funny _____ and it's true, like,
I use YouTube a lot to cook meals and watch, like videos on how to bake something.

3. I hope _____
and I hope you have a wonderful week, with or
without social media.

Retelling WEB動画 💻 DVD

Watch the video again and tell the story of each scene to your partner. You can use the keywords given next to each picture.

e.g.

What Mon decided not to do for a week

> **Keywords**
> social media, touch, see

Model

Mon decided not to use social media for a week. Her rule was that she couldn't touch or see anything related to social media.

1.

What Mon sometimes does with Instagram

> **Keywords**
> inspiration, post, share

2.

Mon's feelings on the last day

> **Keywords**
> integrate, spend, check

Discussion

Q: *Do you think you can stop using all social media for a week? Discuss your ideas with your partner.*

Your ideas	Your partner's ideas

Grammar

Passive Voice

Passive voice, not active voice, is used, for example, when we want to (1) emphasize the receiver of the action, (2) focus on the action, or (3) imply that the agent is unknown, or is not important.

(1) The teacher **is liked** by every student.

The speaker wants to emphasize who every student likes, rather than who likes the teacher.

(2) The decision **was made** to start a new business.

The speaker wants to emphasize the action itself, rather than who took the action.

(3) The window **was broken** yesterday.

The speaker probably doesn't know who broke the window.

Grammar Exercise

Unscramble the following words and complete the sentences.

1. (a group of / the novel / translated / by / experts / was) who have sufficient background knowledge about it.

   _____

2. (conducted / by / the use / smartphones / of / was / the survey / about) the Ministry of Education.

   _____

3. Last week (near / some trees / cut down / were / Ben's house) very suddenly.

   _____

4. It is said that (established / new / within / will / be / a / university) three years in the city.

   _____

5. Many researchers agree that (to / efforts / stabilize / more / made / be / should) the economy.

   _____

6. Although (many years / was / ago / the song / released), it remains very popular among all generations.

   _____

CD 1-06

Instagram is currently one of the most popular social media platforms in the world. There is almost no one who doesn't know the name of this app, but do you know its origin and history? It originated from the creative idea of two young people, and their path to huge success was a long one.

5   The original app was created in 2009 by Kevin Systrom and Mike Krieger. Both of them graduated from Stanford University and interned at Odeo, the predecessor of Twitter. Their success began in a co-working space, where they were working on the development of a new app.

Initially, the app they invented was not called Instagram, but "Burbn." It was designed as a check-in app that allowed users to share their locations and post pictures taken there. However, 10 the app failed to attract users, probably because there was another app that had a similar feature. By analyzing data on the user trends, Kevin and Mike noticed one particular pattern: many of the users posted only their pictures without checking in. They thought the picture filters had something to do with that phenomenon, and therefore decided to focus solely on photos.

Kevin and Mike worked as fast as they could on developing the app. Only eight weeks after 15 they started, at 12:15 a.m. on October 6 in 2010, the new version of the app was launched on the iOS platform. Kevin and Mike renamed the app Instagram, a made-up word combining "instant camera" and "telegram." Instagram rapidly gained popularity, which the founders had not expected. Within a few minutes of its release, the app started to be downloaded by people around the world. It took only a couple of hours for the app to gain more than 10,000 users. By the middle of 20 December that year, the number of registered users increased to one million.

One of the reasons for the app's success may be that it focuses on offering one incredible service, rather than on providing multiple services. Although this kind of decision is occasionally difficult to make, it resulted in the app having over one billion active users today.

Vocabulary Check

Fill in the blanks with the words given in the box. Change the word form if necessary.

1. The _____ of this custom in the village remains unknown.
2. The new model of the car has several improvements over its _____.
3. The event organized by the city succeeded in _____ many people.
4. Using online meeting services has become a global _____.
5. I would like to _____ more knowledge about education.

> attract   origin   phenomenon   gain   predecessor

Reading Comprehension

Answer the following questions.

1. What do the two co-founders have in common?

   _____

2. Why did Burbn fail to be popular?

   _____

3. What did the two co-founders notice through their data analysis?

   _____

4. When did the number of users reach one million?

   _____

Writing

A *Write about your thoughts on sharing aspects of your personal life on social media in 70-80 words, considering the following points.*

❑ Do you think it is a good idea to share aspects of your personal life on social media?

❑ What are the pros of sharing aspects of your personal life on social media?

❑ What are the cons of sharing aspects of your personal life on social media?

B *Make pairs and share your ideas with your partner. Write down what your partner has shared with you.*

Wave Garden

In this unit, you will learn to ...
- focus on the key vocabulary to understand the main idea of the unit.
- identify the meaning of words in context and key terms relating to sports and tourism.
- understand the basic usage of noun phrases postmodified by prepositional phrases.
- express your ideas on sports and tourism based on information in the tasks and activities.

Warming Up

Choose or write your own answers to the following questions. Then ask your partner the questions.

1. How often do you participate in marine sports?
   - ❏ Never
   - ❏ Several times a year
   - ❏ Several times a season
   - ❏ Other ( )

2. What concerns do you have about marine sports?
   - ❏ Safety
   - ❏ Pollution
   - ❏ Cost
   - ❏ Other ( )

3. Which do you prefer, mountains or beaches? And why?

   _____

Watching WEB動画 🖥 💿 DVD 💿 CD 1-07

Watch the video and write a brief outline in approximately five sentences.

Vocabulary 🎧 1-08

A *Choose the most appropriate word from the box to complete the phrases. Change the word form if necessary.*

1. • make _____ waves

   • cause _____ damage to the local society

   • receive _____ support from many people

2. • _____ a garden

   • _____ a sense of compassion

   • _____ a good relationship with friends

3. • _____ a hole

   • _____ through a pile of things

   • _____ deep into the problem

4. • _____ new technology

   • _____ a policy to change education

   • _____ an up-to-date marketing strategy

5. • utilize _____ intelligence

   • produce _____ leather for fashion items

   • transplant an _____ organ into the patient

| cultivate   enormous   artificial   implement   dig |

B *Choose the most appropriate phrase to complete the sentences.*

1. The team _____ losing the game due to their lack of preparation.

   a. ended up

   b. made up

   c. put up

   d. caught up

2. Although he has a lot of responsibilities at work, he always manages to _____.

   a. take the pressure

   b. make the pressure

   c. give the pressure

   d. distribute the pressure

Listening Comprehension WEB動画 📀DVD 🎧CD 1-07

A *Watch the video and choose the correct answers to the following questions.*

1. Where is the "wave garden"?

   a. Wales

   b. England

   c. Scotland

   d. Northern Ireland

2. What does Ali do?

   a. She is a professional surfer.

   b. She is a doctor.

   c. She is a scientist.

   d. She is a teacher.

3. A Spanish company _____.

  a. donated a large amount of money to the wave garden

  b. developed the technology that is applied in the wave garden

  c. conducted several surveys on the ecology of sharks with the wave garden

  d. played a leading role in building the wave garden

B *Answer the following questions.*

1. What does Andy do?

_____

2. What is the size of the lagoon in Surf Snowdonia?

_____

Tips on Listening and Speaking 1-09

Contractions
Contractions are often used in spoken language. A contraction is a shortened form of two words that are combined into one word.

  1. This <u>isn't</u> the first time <u>he's</u> been late for a meeting.
      (is not)   (he has)
  2. <u>I've</u> almost finished my essay, so <u>I'd</u> like you to check it.
   (I have)   (I would)

Dictation 1-10

Listen to the sentences and fill in the blanks.

1. Ali Ward is in Snowdonia _____.

2. The design _____.

3. They were _____ to perfect that.

17

Retelling

WEB動画 DVD

Watch the video again and tell the story of each scene to your partner. You can use the keywords given next to each picture.

e.g.

When Ali met Andy

Keywords

wave garden, enormous, technology

Model

Ali met Andy in the Wave Garden. She asked how these enormous waves are made. Andy talked about the technology used to make the waves.

1.

About the Wave Garden

Keywords

sharks, changing rooms, training ground

2.

The second step for making a wave garden

Keywords

power drill, big secret, water level

Discussion

Q: *Which would you find more attractive, surfing in an artificial park or surfing in the sea? Discuss your ideas with your partner.*

Your ideas	Your partner's ideas

18

Grammar

Noun Phrases Postmodified by Prepositional Phrases

Prepositional phrases can be used if you want to add some more information to a noun phrase.

The apple looks fresh.
The apple <u>on the desk</u> looks fresh.
> *The speaker can describe where **the apple** is.*

That girl is my sister.
That girl <u>with long hair</u> is my sister.
> *The speaker can describe a feature of **that girl**.*

Other examples
Doctors <u>at that hospital</u> are all very kind to patients.
Some people <u>in Canada</u> speak both English and French.

Grammar Exercise

Unscramble the following words and complete the sentences.

1. The beauty (ordinary words / be / the sunset / in / cannot / expressed / of).

   _____

2. (of / a significant influence / the pollution / has / on / rivers and lakes) drinking water quality.

   _____

3. Some university students (in addition to / language / Japan / a / learn / foreign / in) English.

   _____

4. (difficult / to / statistics / the book / about / looks) comprehend.

   _____

5. It might be (individuals / cultural / meaningful / backgrounds / with / encounter / different / to).

   _____

6. The city council members (of / the reconstruction / the plan / the old library / for / discussed).

   _____

CD 1-11

Surfing is one of the most popular marine sports in the world. If you surf, you will receive a considerable number of benefits from it. One of them is arguably feeling a connection with the ocean and nature from a broader perspective. By riding waves in the ocean, surfers can experience the power and beauty of the ocean firsthand, which makes them recognize the importance of
5 conserving the ocean.

Some professional surfers have taken action to tackle environmental problems surrounding the ocean. Among them is Kanoa Igarashi, a world-famous surfer. His remarkable achievements include becoming world champion in 2020 and winning a silver medal in the Tokyo Olympics in 2021. He picks up litter on the beach on a daily basis, motivated by his desire to preserve the
10 charm and attractiveness of the sea. He is currently focused on preserving the ocean for the next generation. On June 8, 2020, World Oceans Day, he posted a message on Instagram to encourage people all over the world to appreciate the beauty of the ocean. He said, "What I love most about the ocean is the fact that it gives us so much and asks for nothing in return."

In 2019, Igarashi became an ambassador of the Shiseido Blue Project, which is organized
15 by Shiseido, a prestigious Japanese company that produces sunscreen. In the news conference, he stated that protecting the sea is more important than obtaining a trophy or a gold medal. In 2023, he participated in an event that was a part of the Shiseido Blue Project. In this event, he was involved in farming kelp, which absorbs and purifies substances that cause pollution in the sea, such as nitrogen or phosphorus.

20 Marine sports are attractive in many ways. However, ongoing ocean pollution could deny future generations the opportunity to enjoy them and recognize their attraction. Although many things have been done to protect the sea, more efforts should be made from the point of view of sustainability.

Vocabulary Check

Fill in the blanks with the words given in the box. Change the word form if necessary.

1. Looking at problems from various _____ often allows us to find a creative solution.
2. We can _____ energy by turning off lights that are not in use.
3. The Nobel Prize is one of the most _____ awards for scholars.
4. The teacher was surprised to see her student's _____ progress.
5. The company appointed a well-known actor as a special _____ to promote their brand.

> perspective   ambassador   remarkable   prestigious   conserve

Reading Comprehension

Answer the following questions.

1. What are some of Igarashi's remarkable achievements?

   _____

2. Why does Igarashi pick up litter on the beach?

   _____

3. What happened to Igarashi in 2019?

   _____

4. What did Igarashi do in the event in 2023?

   _____

21

Writing

A *Write about a unique tourist attraction that enables visitors to feel a connection with nature in 70-80 words, considering the following points.*

❏ Where is the tourist attraction?

❏ What makes it unique?

❏ What season is the best to visit the attraction?

B *Make pairs and share your ideas with your partner. Write down what your partner has shared with you.*

Speaking Through Poetry

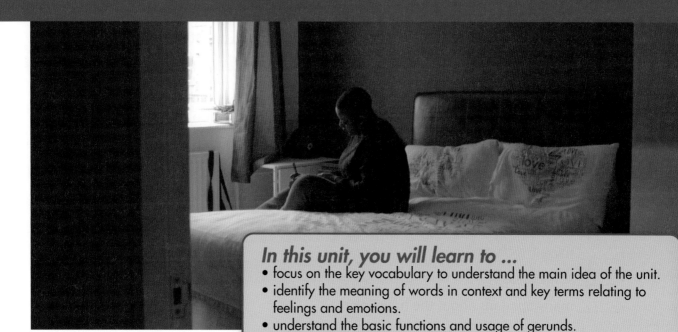

In this unit, you will learn to ...
- focus on the key vocabulary to understand the main idea of the unit.
- identify the meaning of words in context and key terms relating to feelings and emotions.
- understand the basic functions and usage of gerunds.
- express your feelings and emotions using information in the tasks and activities.

Warming Up

Choose or write your own answers to the following questions. Then ask your partner the questions.

1. What do you often do when you feel depressed?
   - ❏ Listen to music
   - ❏ Hang out with friends
   - ❏ Go shopping
   - ❏ Other ( )

2. How often do you write or talk about your feelings?
   - ❏ Every day
   - ❏ Every week
   - ❏ Every month
   - ❏ Other ( )

3. When you were a child, how was your personality? Is it different from your present personality?

   _____

Watching WEB動画 🖥 📀DVD 📀CD 1-12

Watch the video and write a brief outline in approximately five sentences.

23

Vocabulary 🎧 1-13

A *Choose the most appropriate word from the box to complete the phrases. Change the word form if necessary.*

1. • _____ like a child
   • _____ as if nothing happened
   • _____ well

2. • the _____ thing to do
   • be at the _____ stage of the research
   • revise the _____ plan of the project

3. • _____ that swimming is fun
   • _____ a new solution to the problem
   • _____ a secret message behind the speech

4. • _____ innovation
   • _____ the students by giving them positive feedback
   • _____ people to participate in the event

5. • _____ myself
   • _____ some ideas
   • _____ many opinions about the travel plan

| initial   behave   discover   express   encourage |

B *Choose the most appropriate phrasal verb to complete the sentences.*

1. It's important to learn how to _____ difficult feelings.
   a. deal with
   b. break with
   c. go along with
   d. catch up with

2. Before I go shopping, I usually _____ all the items I need.
   a. hand out
   b. set out
   c. make out
   d. write out

Listening Comprehension 📺WEB動画 📀DVD 🎧CD 1-12

A *Watch the video and choose the correct answers to the following questions.*

1. Lucrecia writes poems, when she feels _____.
   a. happy
   b. sad
   c. surprised
   d. dizzy

2. When Lucrecia was young, _____.
   a. she was aggressive toward other people
   b. she was afraid of the adults around her
   c. she was quiet and not talkative
   d. she was good at writing essays

3. What does Lucrecia hope to achieve by sharing her poetry with others?

   a. She wants to become known to them.

   b. She wants to help them feel less alone.

   c. She wants to make money to donate to her hometown.

   d. She wants to receive some feedback from them.

B *Answer the following questions.*

1. What does Lucrecia do first when she writes a poem?

   _____

2. What is the purpose of the charity that Lucrecia helps to run?

   _____

Tips on Listening and Speaking 1-14

Fixed Expressions
Fixed expressions are pronounced as a group together instead of each word being pronounced separately.

   1. Who is in charge of the project?
   2. The bird is a kind of sparrow.

Dictation 1-15

Listen to the sentences and fill in the blanks.

1. This is _____ .

2. She cries _____ .

3. Now Lucrecia _____ to help people through poetry.

25

Retelling WEB動画 📺 🔘 DVD

Watch the video again and tell the story of each scene to your partner. You can use the keywords given next to each picture.

e.g.

A section of one of her poems

> **Keywords**
>
> night, scream, help

Model

In a section of one of her poems, she cries in the middle of the night. She is screaming like Rihanna to ask for someone's help.

1.

Good points of writing

> **Keywords**
>
> discover, a new way, other people

2.

Lucrecia's desire to help people by writing poems

> **Keywords**
>
> caring person, connect, similar situations

Discussion

Q: *Do you want to try to write some poems? And why? Discuss your ideas with your partner.*

Your ideas	Your partner's ideas

Grammar

Gerunds

A gerund is a form of verb + -ing that functions as a noun in a sentence. Gerunds are used, for example, as sentential subjects and objects of verbs or prepositions.

<u>Expressing your own feelings to others</u> is important.
This gerund functions as the sentential subject.

Cindy always enjoys <u>performing dance with her friends</u>.
This gerund functions as the object of the verb "enjoy."

Some people are not good at <u>making a speech in front of a large audience</u>.
This gerund functions as the object of the preposition "at."

Grammar Exercise

Unscramble the following words and complete the sentences.

1. (clarifying / change / climate / of / the mechanism / needs) a lot of time.

   _____

2. (to play / the skill / mastering / instrument / musical / a) is a long process.

   _____

3. Workers (confidential / avoid / data / highly / should / viewing) outside their company.

   _____

4. The city government (postpone / details / decided / announcing / to / the charity event / about) for safety reasons.

   _____

5. It is better (from / refrain / to / on / talking / the phone) when you are on the train.

   _____

6. The professor (of / herself / dedicated / to / the quality / improving / has / education) for all people.

   _____

Anger is a natural emotion that everyone sometimes experiences on a daily basis. It can be triggered by various factors such as stress, frustration, fear, or disappointment. While feeling angry is normal, it is important to learn how to manage anger in a healthy way if you aim to live a better life. Recently, much
5 attention has been paid to anger management by a variety of people with different backgrounds.

Anger management refers to the process of recognizing, understanding, and controlling one's anger to prevent it from causing harm to oneself or others. The goal of anger management is not to suppress or eliminate the feelings of
10 anger, because anger is an innate emotion that plays an important role in self-protection. Rather, anger management is a technique that aims to equip people with the skills to manage their emotional and physical responses to anger in a constructive manner. There are a wide range of anger management techniques, including learning to think about something in an objective manner, waiting for
15 six seconds after a moment that makes you angry, or just taking a deep breath.

One way to manage your anger is to keep an "anger diary," which may help you identify in what situations you feel anger. Knowing about yourself, in terms of what situations provoke you, may enable you to keep your temper under control. When you keep an anger diary, it is considered ideal to record as
20 many details as possible in order to identify some specific factors that make you irritated. For example, you can record not only what happened and what you felt at that moment, but also how your body responded to the situation, or whether you already felt pressure about something else such as work or human relationships.

25 It is not possible for us to avoid anger, which is inherent in human emotions. However, when we are unable to manage it effectively, it can lead to negative outcomes. Learning how to manage anger may reduce the negative impact that anger has on our everyday lives and lead us to live in a healthier and more fulfilling way.

Vocabulary Check

Fill in the blanks with the words given in the box. Change the word form if necessary.

1. His _____ sense of humor always makes people around him laugh.

2. The professor gave some _____ comments on the student's essay.

3. The boy's aggressive attitude toward his little brother _____ his parents last weekend.

4. Completing a full marathon was one of the most _____ experiences in my life.

5. Tom tried to _____ his nervousness before the final presentation of the course.

| provoke | fulfilling | innate | constructive | suppress |

Reading Comprehension

Answer the following questions.

1. How is anger caused? Give some examples.

_____

2. What is anger management?

_____

3. What are some techniques of anger management?

_____

4. How can keeping an anger diary be helpful?

_____

Writing

A *Write about an experience that made you feel a specific emotion in 70-80 words, considering the following points.*

❏ What feelings did you have during that experience?

❏ What made you have those feelings?

❏ How did the experience influence your present self?

B *Make pairs and share your ideas with your partner. Write down what your partner has shared with you.*

Cooking Korean

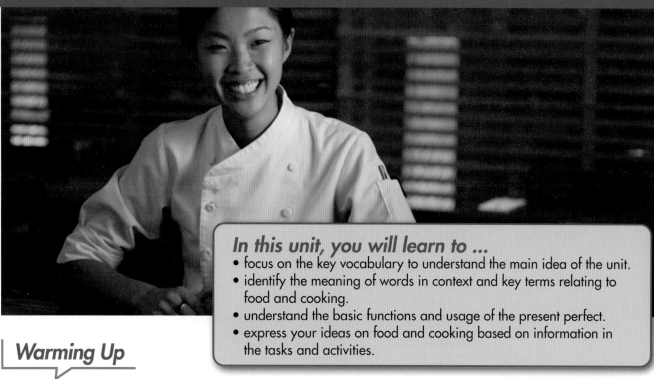

In this unit, you will learn to ...
* focus on the key vocabulary to understand the main idea of the unit.
* identify the meaning of words in context and key terms relating to food and cooking.
* understand the basic functions and usage of the present perfect.
* express your ideas on food and cooking based on information in the tasks and activities.

Warming Up

Choose or write your own answers to the following questions. Then ask your partner the questions.

1. What kind of food do you like?
   ❑ Japanese food　　　　　　　❑ French food
   ❑ Chinese food　　　　　　　❑ Other (　　　　　　　　　　　)

2. What kind of Korean food have you ever eaten?
   ❑ Kimchi (spicy fermented vegetables)　❑ Samgyeopsal (gilled pork belly)
   ❑ Bibimbap (mixed rice with vegetables, meat, and egg)
   ❑ Other (　　　　　　　　　　　)

3. Which do you prefer, cooking at home or eating out? And why?

_____

Watching　WEB動画 🖥️ 📀 DVD 💿 CD 1-17

Watch the video and write a brief outline in approximately five sentences.

Vocabulary 🎧 1-18

A *Choose the most appropriate word from the box to complete the phrases. Change the word form if necessary.*

1. • _____ butter on toast
   • _____ into a crowd
   • _____ my heart

2. • cook American _____
   • enjoy _____ at a local restaurant
   • prepare _____ for the party

3. • achieve an _____ relationship with the company
   • have an _____ impact on the economy
   • make an _____ discovery

4. • _____ some water into the cup
   • _____ a glass of wine
   • _____ all my energy into the project

5. • learn about _____ food from local people
   • eat _____ Italian pizza
   • experience _____ Japanese culture

cuisine	pour	melt	incredible	authentic

B *Choose the most appropriate meaning of the underlined expressions.*

1. Lunch is ready. Time to <u>dig in</u>.
   a. wash hands
   b. start eating
   c. take a break
   d. clean up

2. I cooked miso soup for dinner, and it <u>turned out</u> very good.
   a. became
   b. finished
   c. changed
   d. ended

Listening Comprehension 💻 📀 🎧 1-17

A *Watch the video and choose the correct answers to the following questions.*

1. Kristen is a chef specializing in _____.
   a. French food
   b. Spanish food
   c. Japanese food
   d. Chinese food

2. Danielle asks the server in the cafe _____.
   a. how to order the food
   b. how to make the food
   c. how to spell the name of the food
   d. how to pronounce the name of the food

3. Which of the following is true of Kristen?

 a. She thinks the Korean-style donut is too sweet for her.

 b. She has cooked Korean food with Danielle several times.

 c. She wants to go to Korea to master Korean food.

 d. She hopes to feel people's passion for Korean food.

B *Answer the following questions.*

1. Where was Kristen born?

_____

2. What does Maangchi show Danielle?

_____

Tips on Listening and Speaking 🎧 1-19

Adverbs Expressing Certainty
Some adverbs are used to indicate a strong sense of agreement, affirmation, or confirmation. They are often used to emphasize the speaker's conviction or certainty about something.

 1. I will definitely be there on time. (*"Definitely" is used to express certainty here.*)
 2. Certainly, I can help you with that project. (*"Certainly" is used to express polite agreement or response here.*)
 3. The movie was absolutely fantastic. (*"Absolutely" is used to express emphasis here.*)

Dictation 🎧 1-20

Listen to the sentences and fill in the blanks.

1. Danielle Chang loves Asian food and she wants _____.

2. Danielle and Kristen agree _____ in downtown New York.

3. Hi, we're _____, we've heard so much about them.

33

Retelling

WEB動画 DVD

Watch the video again and tell the story of each scene to your partner. You can use the keywords given next to each picture.

e.g.

Danielle and Kristen when and after the Korean donuts were served

Keywords

server,　how to eat,　incredible

Model

Danielle asked the server how to eat the Korean donut. The server then answered they could eat it in any way they liked. Kristen and Danielle thought that the donut was incredible.

1.

Kristen's background

Keywords

be born,　be adopted,　cooking

2.

The procedure of cooking kimchi in the video

Keywords

tear,　bite-sized,　pour

Discussion

Q: *What are possible advantages of learning about food that is popular in other cultures? Discuss your ideas with your partner.*

Your ideas	Your partner's ideas

Grammar

Present Perfect for Describing an Experience

The present perfect tense can be used to describe past experiences or events that still have some influence on the present moment.

Martin <u>has visited</u> Toronto three times.
> *The speaker can express that Martin has the experience of visiting Toronto three times.*

Some words such as "before" or "ever" are used together with the present perfect tense in order to make the usage clear.
I have visited Beijing <u>before</u>, though I'm not sure how many times I have been there.
Have you <u>ever</u> visited Yokohama?

Grammar Exercise

Unscramble the following words and complete the sentences.

1. Emma (twenty / her lifetime / more than / visited / in / has / countries).

_____

2. The explorer (animals / the jungle / exceptionally / in / has / rare / encountered) before.

_____

3. The actor (movies / a lot of / has / in / world-famous / appeared).

_____

4. Have (participated / experiment / ever / in / you / psychological / a)?

_____

5. Ken (cuisine / never / authentic / eaten / has / French), so he really wants the chance.

_____

6. We (kimchi / several / scratch / have / from / made) times.

_____

🎵 1-21

Kimchi, which consists of salted and fermented vegetables with various kinds of seasonings, is one of the most famous traditional Korean dishes. It is not only an important part of Korean food culture, but also a symbol of identity for Korean people. Kimchi is currently highly popular all over the world as well. Its history dates back to ancient times thousands of years ago.

5   Your image of kimchi may be that it is red and spicy. However, the original version of kimchi that had been made for a long time in the past was quite different from what it is today. Korean people are said to have started to produce kimchi over 3,000 years ago, as a way to store vegetables for the cold winter when they faced the prospect of starvation. At that time, because chili pepper was not used, kimchi was not red and spicy.

10   According to one account, it was not until the 16th century that chili pepper began to be used to make kimchi. After some time, a variety of seasonings were gradually introduced into the production of kimchi, thereby shaping it into its modern form. Interestingly, napa cabbage kimchi, the most popular type of kimchi, became widespread relatively recently, between the end of the 19th century and the beginning of the 20th century. Until then, other vegetables such as eggplant,
15 radish, or cucumber had been used as the main ingredients.

     Today, kimchi is enjoyed in various forms by many people around the world. It is estimated that there are more than 200 types in Korea, including kkakdugi (cubed radish kimchi), mul kimchi (water kimchi), and chonggak kimchi (ponytail radish kimchi). In addition, it is used in many dishes as an important ingredient, such as kimchi fried rice, kimchi pancakes, and kimchi stew.

20   The history of kimchi is a reflection of Korean culture and its evolution over time. From its humble beginnings as a simple method of preserving vegetables, kimchi has become a beloved dish that represents the identity of Korean people. Its popularity may continue to grow, as more people become aware of its attractions.

Vocabulary Check

Fill in the blanks with the words given in the box. Change the word form if necessary.

1. _____ food is believed to have many health benefits.

2. I prefer to use a mix of different _____ to make food tasty.

3. We need to _____ this historically significant building for future generations.

4. More efforts should be made to decrease the number of people who die from _____.

5. The _____ use of smartphones has changed the way of our communication.

| widespread | preserve | seasoning | starvation | fermented |

Reading Comprehension

Answer the following questions.

1. Why did Korean people start making kimchi?

   _____

2. When is it thought that chili pepper started being used in making kimchi?

   _____

3. When did napa kimchi become common?

   _____

4. How many types of kimchi are there in Korea today?

   _____

Writing

A *If you could attend a class where you can learn both a language and cooking at the same time, what country or region would you choose? Write about the class in 70-80 words, considering the following points.*

❑ What makes you interested in that country or region?
❑ Do you have any specific food that you would like to cook?
❑ Would you prefer individual lessons or group lessons?

Useful Expressions

I am interested in learning how to cook French food, because …
I have a strong interest in Korean food. One reason is that …
Participating in individual lessons is more attractive to me, because …
Compared to individual lessons, group lessons are …
Group lessons are more fascinating than individual lessons in that …

Useful Vocabulary

make something from scratch   cook authentic dishes   learn from a culinary expert
interact with other participants   deepen understanding of the culture

B *Make pairs and share your ideas with your partner. Write down what your partner has shared with you.*

My Favorite Places

In this unit, you will learn to ...
- focus on the key vocabulary to understand the main idea of the unit.
- identify the meaning of words in context and key terms relating to preferences.
- understand the basic usage of noun phrases postmodified by relative clauses.
- express your own preferences and reasons for them based on information in the tasks and activities.

Warming Up

Choose or write your own answers to the following questions. Then ask your partner the questions.

1. What kind of place do you like to visit?
   ❏ A place where you can experience thrills   ❏ A place where you can relax
   ❏ A place where you can see beautiful scenery   ❏ Other ( )

2. When you feel stressed, what do you do?
   ❏ Go to your favorite places   ❏ Talk with your friends
   ❏ Listen to music   ❏ Other ( )

3. Do you like to go outside or stay indoors? Why?

Watching

WEB動画 🖥️ 📀 DVD 💿 CD 1-22

Watch the video and write a brief outline in approximately five sentences.

Vocabulary

🎧 1-23

A *Choose the most appropriate word from the box to complete the phrases. Change the word form if necessary.*

1. • finally complete the _____ job
   • work under physically _____ conditions
   • avoid _____ situations

2. • be _____ to the doctor
   • be _____ for support
   • feel _____ to be alive

3. • _____ money on clothes
   • _____ too much time inside
   • _____ weeks completing the project

4. • _____ me of the importance of nature
   • _____ the student about the deadline for the report
   • _____ me that every one of us is important

5. • the cutting _____
   • the sharp _____
   • the _____ of the world

| remind stressful spend edge grateful |

B *Choose the most appropriate meaning of each idiom given below.*

1. take one's breath away
   a. make someone sleepy
   b. cause someone to feel fatigue
   c. impress someone greatly
   d. hurt someone on purpose

2. fuel the imagination
   a. do something with confidence
   b. encourage creative thinking
   c. create something imaginary
   d. limit the potential

Listening Comprehension

WEB動画 🖥 DVD 🎧 1-22

A *Watch the video and choose the correct answers to the following questions.*

1. Why does Ben like Lake Ontario?
   a. Because he likes to watch the sunset in the evening.
   b. Because he loves to walk on the rocks.
   c. Because he lives near the lake and can often go there.
   d. Because he can enjoy fishing there.

2. With whom does Ben usually go to Arthur's Seat?
   a. With his family
   b. With his colleague
   c. With his friend
   d. All by himself

3. What makes Ben grateful to be alive?

    a. Traveling to different places

    b. Watching sunsets

    c. Having many people around

    d. Being outside in nature

B *Answer the following questions.*

1. When Ben gets stressed, what does he like to do?

_____

2. Inspired by making this video, what is Ben going to do?

_____

Tips on Listening and Speaking   🎧 1-24

Linking ([t] sound + vowel)
When one word ends with the [t] sound and the next word starts with a vowel, these sounds are linked in pronunciation.

    1. Don't worry about it.
             about it → abou-tit

    2. Let's meet at eight.
           meet at eight → mee-ta-teight

Dictation   🎧 1-25

Listen to the sentences and fill in the blanks.

1. I love the sound of the waves and I _____.

2. _____ is the city of Toronto catching the sunlight.

3. _____, I like to go to Edinburgh and climb Arthur's Seat.

41

Retelling

Watch the video again and tell the story of each scene to your partner. You can use the keywords given next to each picture.

e.g.

West Palm Beach

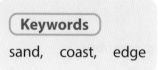

Keywords

sand, coast, edge

Model

One of Ben's favorite places is West Palm Beach. It's in South Florida, in the United States. Ben thinks that the sand of West Palm Beach is very beautiful. He also feels that standing on the coast is like standing at the edge of the world.

1.

Lake Ontario

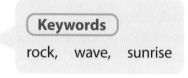

Keywords

rock, wave, sunrise

2.

Arthur's Seat

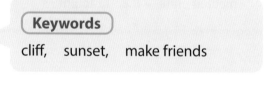

Keywords

cliff, sunset, make friends

Discussion

Q: *Which place do you want to visit, West Palm Beach, Lake Ontario, or Arthur's Seat? Does it change depending on your purpose? Discuss your ideas with your partner.*

Your ideas	Your partner's ideas

Grammar

Noun Phrases Postmodified by Relative Clauses

Relative clauses can be used to add some more information to noun phrases. There are two basic types of relative clauses: subject relative clauses and object relative clauses.

Subject relative clauses

The woman is a lawyer.

The woman <u>who lives next door</u> is a lawyer.

The speaker can express that the woman lives next door.

Object relative clauses

The hat is nice.

The hat <u>that my father often wears</u> is nice.

The speaker can express that the speaker's father often wears the hat.

Grammar Exercise

Unscramble the following words and complete the sentences.

1. This is (that / London / the picture / in / took / my cousin).

   _____

2. In Japan, there (many children / have / are / their / who / own / smartphone).

   _____

3. (customer / the document / submitted / our / that / just) should be revised.

   _____

4. (last / that / opened / the new café / month) is now very popular among young people.

   _____

5. Taylor (her / that / the support / offer / appreciates / friends) to her.

   _____

6. (that / designed / a famous architect / was / the bridge / by) is the symbol of the city.

   _____

43

🎧 1-26

Do you have any places that you like to visit? Going to your favorite places might provide you with different types of benefits. Regular trips to your favorite places can help you reduce stress and anxiety, increase feelings of contentment, and strengthen human relationships.

Our favorite places are often associated with special memories with family members or
5　friends. For instance, if you revisit a place where your parents took you when you were young, you can recall the enjoyment of those bygone days and recognize how much your parents loved you. This kind of experience may make the bond with your parents even stronger.

Some people like to visit quiet places because they can concentrate on a task such as completing a school assignment, composing a new song, or reading a book. Quiet places may
10　calm them mentally and promote logical or creative thinking. Furthermore, if thinking in this kind of setting helps us achieve something, that achievement may seem even more fulfilling.

Another significant thing about visiting a favorite place is that it relaxes us. Just going there can help reduce stress and maintain good mental health. The effectiveness of visiting one's favorite places was examined in an experimental study. This study compared two groups: members in the
15　experimental group visited their favorite places every weekday, and those in the control group visited their favorite places one time a week or not at all. The results suggest that the members of the experimental group felt more comfortable and energetic compared to the control group. In other words, visiting one's favorite places may be a good coping strategy as far as mental health is concerned.

20　In conclusion, you may gain various kinds of benefits through visiting your favorite places. Try to go there when you have time, or even when you are tied up with other things. If you cannot get there easily, just close your eyes and think of that place, just as Ben does in the video.

Vocabulary Check

Fill in the blanks with the words given in the box. Change the word form if necessary.

1. Regular exercise may help _____ your risk of heart disease.
2. The government should _____ the importance of education.
3. People cannot make a _____ decision when they are sleepy and tired.
4. The uncertainty of the future is one of the main sources of _____ for many people.
5. After taking a rest for a couple of days, Tom finally felt _____.

| logical | energetic | recognize | anxiety | reduce |

Reading Comprehension

Answer the following questions.

1. How can you recall your childhood days?

   _____

2. Why do some people like to go to quiet places?

   _____

3. How often did the participants of the experimental group visit their favorite places?

   _____

4. What should you do if it's difficult to physically visit your favorite place?

   _____

Writing

A *Write about your favorite place in 70-80 words, considering the following points.*

❏ Where is your favorite place?
❏ Why do you like the place?
❏ What is the most impressive thing that you have ever experienced there?

B *Make pairs and share your ideas with your partner. Write down what your partner has shared with you.*

46

British Sign Language

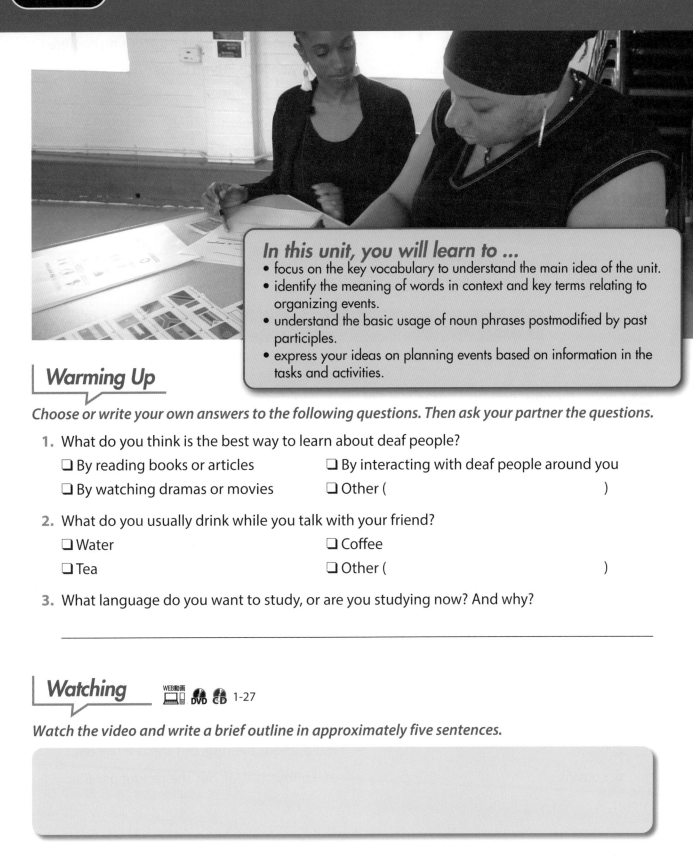

In this unit, you will learn to ...
- focus on the key vocabulary to understand the main idea of the unit.
- identify the meaning of words in context and key terms relating to organizing events.
- understand the basic usage of noun phrases postmodified by past participles.
- express your ideas on planning events based on information in the tasks and activities.

Warming Up

Choose or write your own answers to the following questions. Then ask your partner the questions.

1. What do you think is the best way to learn about deaf people?
   - ❏ By reading books or articles
   - ❏ By interacting with deaf people around you
   - ❏ By watching dramas or movies
   - ❏ Other (   )

2. What do you usually drink while you talk with your friend?
   - ❏ Water
   - ❏ Coffee
   - ❏ Tea
   - ❏ Other (   )

3. What language do you want to study, or are you studying now? And why?

   _____

Watching   WEB動画 🖥️ 📀 DVD 💿 CD 1-27

Watch the video and write a brief outline in approximately five sentences.

Vocabulary 🎧 1-28

A *Choose the most appropriate word from the box to complete the phrases. Change the word form if necessary.*

1. • _____ a party

   • _____ a project team

   • _____ an exhibition of art works

2. • _____ for the event

   • _____ a presentation for the upcoming conference

   • _____ my child to attend university

3. • have a _____ with friends

   • dislike a one-sided _____

   • keep a _____ going

4. • _____ the rules of the game

   • _____ the symptoms to the doctor

   • _____ the reason for the major restructuring

5. • solve the _____

   • cause many _____

   • have no _____ understanding each other

> prepare   organize   conversation   problem   explain

B *Choose the most appropriate meaning of the underlined expressions.*

1. I'd like to <u>get along</u> with my colleague.

   a. get away

   b. get by

   c. get back

   d. get on

2. <u>Well done</u>, Mike!

   a. Nice try

   b. Good luck

   c. Excellent job

   d. No problem

Listening Comprehension 📺 WEB動画 💿 DVD 🎧 1-27

A *Watch the video and choose the correct answers to the following questions.*

1. Dionne and La Toya are _____.

   a. classmates

   b. friends

   c. sisters

   d. cousins

2. What is true about Dionne and La Toya?

   a. Dionne is hearing, but she can use BSL.

   b. Dionne is deaf, but she cannot use BSL.

   c. La Toya is hearing, but she can use BSL.

   d. La Toya is deaf, but she cannot use BSL.

3. In BSL, sentences should be _____.

    a. short and direct

    b. short and indirect

    c. long and direct

    d. long and indirect

B *Answer the following questions.*

1. What is important for learning any language?

    _____

2. How does La Toya believe learning should be?

    _____

Tips on Listening and Speaking   🔊 1-29

Avoid Making Definitive Statements

In speaking, some expressions are used to avoid making definitive statements so that you can express that there may be different interpretations.

    1. <u>It looks like</u> all my classmates like our English classes.
    2. That <u>may not be the best way</u> to do that.
    3. She <u>seems to</u> misunderstand the purpose of this project.

Dictation   🔊 1-30

Listen to the sentences and fill in the blanks.

1. Tea, biscuits, a few other snacks, and a chat. Dionne and La Toya think this is

    _____.

2. And that's exactly what _____ to do.

3. After tea, food, and games, it looks like _____.

Retelling

WEB動画 DVD

Watch the video again and tell the story of each scene to your partner. You can use the keywords given next to each picture.

e.g.

About the party Dionne and La Toya are organizing

Keywords

practice, BSL, hearing and deaf

Model

The purpose of the party was to practice BSL. Dionne and La Toya wanted to invite both hearing and deaf people to the party.

1.

Features of BSL

Keywords

different, speak, visual

2.

What the party was like

Keywords

should be fun, explain the rules, the same accent

Discussion

Q: *If you were to organize a party like the one in this video, what would you do? Discuss your ideas with your partner.*

Your ideas	Your partner's ideas

Grammar

Noun Phrases Postmodified by Past Participles

Past participles can be used to add some more information to noun phrases.

The picture is beautiful.

The picture <u>taken by my mother</u> is beautiful.

> *The speaker can express that the picture was taken by the speaker's mother.*

The car is known for its reliability.

The car <u>manufactured in Japan</u> is known for its reliability.

> *The speaker can express that the car was manufactured in Japan.*

Make sure you keep a copy of the document.

Make sure you keep a copy of the document <u>signed by the CEO</u>.

> *The speaker can express that the document was signed by the CEO.*

Grammar Exercise

Unscramble the following words and complete the sentences.

1. (the museum / will / by / be / every year / visited / many people) closed next year.

   _____

2. (has / written / been / a famous author / the book / by) translated into many languages.

   _____

3. (suggested / the plan / by / during / the president / the meeting / was) not realistic.

   _____

4. The researcher disproved (one / formulated / the economic theories / of / ago / some decades).

   _____

5. Last week John and Ben (a sports event / participated in / by / organized / the local community).

   _____

6. Yesterday we (went to / in / recommended / a restaurant / about Italian cuisine / a TV program).

   _____

51

Have you ever heard of the acronym "CODA"?

CODA, which stands for children of deaf adults, refers to hearing children who are born to deaf parents. It is said that more than 90 percent of deaf adults are known to have children with
5 normal hearing ability. Some researchers point out that CODA often experience certain types of challenges due to the fact that they grow up in two culturally, socially, and linguistically different communities: the deaf community and the hearing community.

10   One of the main difficulties CODA may face is related to communication. As their parents use sign language as their means of communication, they are exposed to natural input of sign language from very early ages. As a result, they may acquire the sign language their parents use. In some families, however, deaf parents do not use sign language to communicate with their hearing children, preferring to use spoken language, which can
15 lead to restricted parent-child communication. Additionally, since they have fewer opportunities for verbal communication in comparison with children raised in hearing families, some delays are usually observed in CODA's spoken language development.

     CODA frequently play an important role in bridging the gap between the deaf and hearing communities. They help their parents understand the culture of the hearing
20 community in many ways. Such experiences may foster maturity, independence, and stronger relationships with their parents. On the other hand, CODA sometimes feel overwhelmed and burdened when serving as an interpreter or communicator for their parents, for example, when the content of what they interpret is not age-appropriate. They may feel guilty about refusing to go along with their parents' requests despite not being
25 comfortable with what they are asked to do.

     In our society, there are some people who are facing challenges that we are not very familiar with, and CODA might be an example of this. It is crucial for us to attempt to broaden our understanding of these challenges and explore ways to provide support to those people if we are attempting to realize an inclusive society.

Vocabulary Check

Fill in the blanks with the words given in the box. Change the word form if necessary.

1. Judy was determined to _____ new skills for her future career.

2. The Italian restaurant has a _____ menu due to the shortage of ingredients.

3. My son showed _____ by doing his homework all by himself.

4. Unfortunately, I had to _____ the invitation for my close friend's wedding because of a sudden business trip.

5. We need to _____ an optimal solution to the problem.

> acquire   explore   refuse   independence   restricted

Reading Comprehension

Answer the following questions.

1. What is the definition of CODA?

   _____

2. Why do CODA experience challenges?

   _____

3. What is a language-related problem in some deaf families?

   _____

4. What are some positive traits CODA may develop from their experiences?

   _____

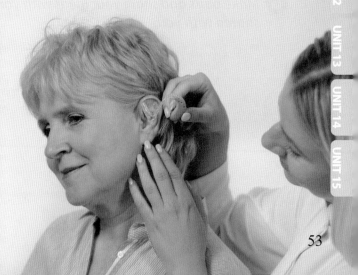

Writing

A *Write about an event that should be organized for the purpose of building an inclusive community in 70-80 words, considering the following points.*

❑ What kind of event should be organized?

❑ Who does the event target?

❑ What behaviors should be recommended or avoided in the event?

B *Make pairs and share your ideas with your partner. Write down what your partner has shared with you.*

E-body

In this unit, you will learn to ...
- focus on the key vocabulary to understand the main idea of the unit.
- identify the meaning of words in context and key terms relating to technology.
- understand various usages of the verb *make*.
- describe how technology is applied to various products or services based on information in the tasks and activities.

Warming Up

Choose or write your own answers to the following questions. Then ask your partner the questions.

1. When you are busy, how do you calm yourself down?
   - ❏ Read books
   - ❏ Listen to music
   - ❏ Go to a park
   - ❏ Other ( )

2. What do you think is most important for communication with others?
   - ❏ Eye contact
   - ❏ Empathy
   - ❏ Patience
   - ❏ Other ( )

3. What kind of technology do you use in your daily communication?

_____

Watching WEB動画 🖥️ DVD 💿 CD 1-32

Watch the video and write a brief outline in approximately five sentences.

Vocabulary 🎧 1-33

A *Choose the most appropriate word from the box to complete the phrases. Change the word form if necessary.*

1. • need _____ support from someone
   • promote children's _____ development
   • improve physical and _____ health

2. • become _____ of my parents
   • work as an _____ consultant
   • want to be _____ from technology

3. • _____ emergency situations
   • _____ complex problems
   • _____ sensitive issues

4. • have no _____ for the medicine
   • try to find a _____ for the manager
   • use honey as a _____ for sugar

5. • investigate the cause of _____
   • be diagnosed with _____
   • ask the doctor about _____

| handle   independent   emotional   substitute   autism |

B *Choose the most appropriate phrasal verb to complete the sentences.*

1. When you feel angry at someone, take a deep breath and try to _____.
   a. calm down
   b. break down
   c. put down
   d. cut down

2. John closed the window to _____ the noise of the traffic outside.
   a. figure out
   b. work out
   c. point out
   d. block out

Listening Comprehension 📺 📀 🎧 1-32

A *Watch the video and choose the correct answers to the following questions.*

1. According to some scientists, how many hugs are needed for your survival?
   a. Three hugs a day
   b. Four hugs a day
   c. Three hugs a week
   d. Four hugs a week

2. The "T-Jacket" is a jacket that _____.
   a. gives people the sensation of a hug
   b. motivates people to have hugs with others
   c. keeps you cool even in hot weather
   d. encourages people to live without hugs

3. Which of the following is true about Julie's son?

    a. He does not like to be hugged.

    b. He is very sensitive to sights and sounds around him.

    c. He felt stressed after he used the T-Jacket.

    d. He didn't want to wear the T-Jacket at first.

B *Answer the following questions.*

1. In what country is the presenter in this video?

    _____

2. Why does Julie think her son should be independent?

    _____

Tips on Listening and Speaking 1-34

Linking ([ch] + vowel)
When the final sound of a word is the [ch] sound and the initial sound of the next word is a vowel, these sounds are pronounced as being linked.

    1. We're going to wat<u>ch a</u> movie tonight.
                watch a → wat-cha
    2. In this hospital, lun<u>ch is</u> served to patients at 12:30.
                lunch is → lun-chis

Dictation 1-35

Listen to the sentences and fill in the blanks.

1. Do not fear me. I am only here to give out hugs. _____!

2. He believes _____ to our emotional well-being.

3. As Julie can't always be around, the T-Jacket might just be _____ _____.

Retelling

WEB動画

DVD

Watch the video again and tell the story of each scene to your partner. You can use the keywords given next to each picture.

e.g.

The purpose of Justin's visit to Singapore

Keywords

power,　hugs,　trust

Model

Justin visited Singapore to find out about the power of hugs. He talked with Dr. James Teh about the power of hugs. Dr. Teh thinks that touch is very powerful, and it communicates trust, love, emotions, and a sense of assurance.

1.

The role of Julie's hugs for her son

Keywords

be easily overstimulated,　stressful moments, by one's side

2.

How to use the T-jacket

Keywords

app,　smartphone,　inflate

Discussion

Q: *Like the T-jacket, the development of science and technology can contribute to the improvement of some people's daily lives. Are there any other examples? Discuss your ideas with your partner.*

Your ideas	Your partner's ideas

58

Grammar

Various Usages of "Make"

The verb "make" is used in various types of constructions.

(1) My aunt made me Korean food. (S+V+O+O)

(2) The birthday present from my parents made me happy. (S+V+O+C, C = adjective)

(3) My favorite singer's songs always make me feel energetic. (S+V+O+C, C = verb)

(4) I want to make our office a comfortable place for everyone. (S+V+O+C, C = noun)

Grammar Exercise

Unscramble the following words and complete the sentences.

1. The teacher (solve / problems / made / difficult / math / the students).

   _____

2. Judy (her colleague / made / an offer / as / work / to) a project leader.

   _____

3. The advice (more passionate / the student / made / the professor / from) about research.

   _____

4. The researcher hopes to (make / improving / for / a useful tool / technology / the quality) of our daily lives.

   _____

5. The politician's words (how / about / to / reform / made / education / citizens / uncomfortable).

   _____

6. The boss (made / more detailed / look up / Kate / the client / about / information).

   _____

59

あしらせ

🎧 1-36

Technology has enriched our daily lives dramatically. Nowadays, almost everybody has their own smartphone. We cannot imagine living without the Internet. In this way, we rely heavily on the advancement of technology. Although human beings have developed various types of technology, more significant is how it is applied in our everyday lives. Technology should play a
5 more important role in providing support to those who have specific difficulties in their daily lives, thereby realizing a more inclusive society. A growing number of services have been created as a result of applying advanced technology.

One example is "Ashirase," a service for people with visual impairment developed by a Japanese man whose visually impaired relative was involved in a pedestrian accident. People with
10 visual impairment need to process a lot of information, particularly when visiting a place for the first time. They have to follow instructions to get to their destination by listening to navigation from their smartphone. At the same time, in order to stay safe, they must pay attention to the sounds around them as well as the sensation of their feet. Such difficulties cause a lot of stress to people with visual impairment, which discourages them from going out, even when they want to.

15 Ashirase was invented to support such people. It offers a service that guides visually impaired people to their destination by generating vibrations in the shoes they wear. After users set a destination using the app, the device attached to their shoes can tell them how to get there, by changing the patterns of the vibration. For example, when they need to turn left, only the left shoe will vibrate. When they are going the right way, both the right and left shoe vibrate simultaneously
20 to let them confirm this. One user said, "I was able to go to the convenience store all by myself for the first time." This service is arguably of great help for those who have visual impairment.

Now, many other innovative services have been invented for helping people with specific difficulties overcome the challenges they may face. Advances in technology are not only for improving our daily lives. Their value also lies in making equal opportunities accessible to every
25 individual in the world, irrespective of their circumstances.

60

Vocabulary Check

Fill in the blanks with the words given in the box. Change the word form if necessary.

1. Reading books is an effective way to _____ your vocabulary.
2. When you have a difficult time, you can _____ on your friends.
3. It is important for drivers to be careful of _____.
4. Jonathan came up with an _____ solution to the company's computer problems.
5. The team managed to _____ various obstacles and complete the project successfully.

> rely   enrich   innovative   pedestrian   overcome

Reading Comprehension

Answer the following questions.

1. Who invented Ashirase?

   _____

2. What must people with visual impairments pay attention to when going to their destination?

   _____

3. How does Ashirase guide its users to their destination?

   _____

4. When users of Ashirase go in the right direction, how does Ashirase let them know?

   _____

あしらせ

Writing

A *Write about a scientific or technological product or service that you would like to invent for people with specific difficulties in 70-80 words, considering the following points.*

❏ What are the product or service's distinctive features?
❏ Who are the target users?
❏ How would your product or service be helpful for these people?

Useful Expressions

I would like to invent a product that can …
The service is different from other existing ones in that …
The service is mainly for …
The product may be helpful for …
By using the service, it would be possible to …

Useful Vocabulary

apply the latest technology   develop a new app   utilize artificial intelligence
help elderly people walk smoothly   support children with learning disabilities

B *Make pairs and share your ideas with your partner. Write down what your partner has shared with you.*

Swimming With Whales

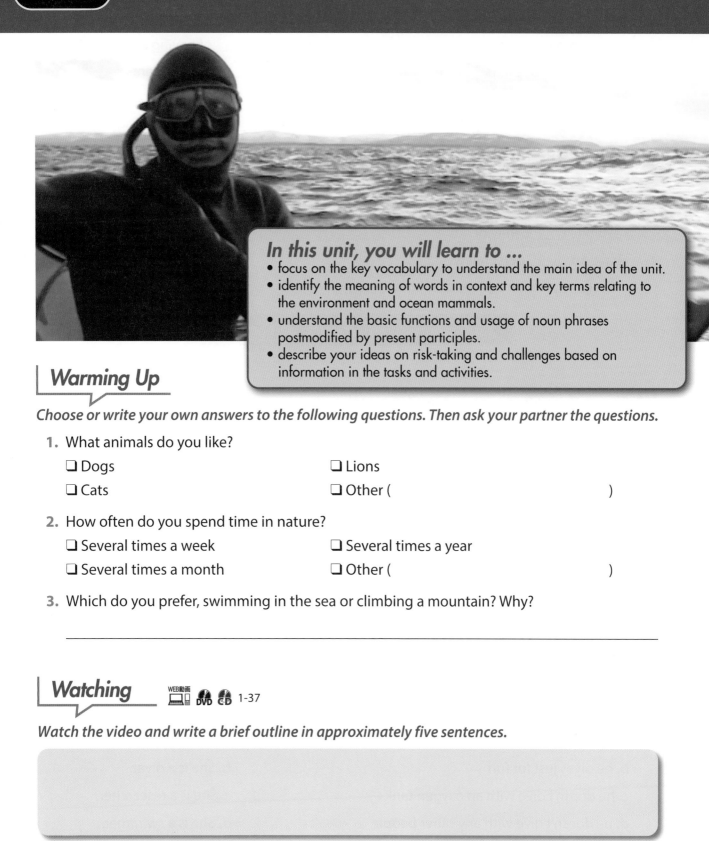

In this unit, you will learn to ...
- focus on the key vocabulary to understand the main idea of the unit.
- identify the meaning of words in context and key terms relating to the environment and ocean mammals.
- understand the basic functions and usage of noun phrases postmodified by present participles.
- describe your ideas on risk-taking and challenges based on information in the tasks and activities.

Warming Up

Choose or write your own answers to the following questions. Then ask your partner the questions.

1. What animals do you like?
   ❏ Dogs   ❏ Lions
   ❏ Cats   ❏ Other (   )

2. How often do you spend time in nature?
   ❏ Several times a week   ❏ Several times a year
   ❏ Several times a month   ❏ Other (   )

3. Which do you prefer, swimming in the sea or climbing a mountain? Why?

   _____

Watching

WEB動画 DVD CD 1-37

Watch the video and write a brief outline in approximately five sentences.

Vocabulary 🎧 1-38

A *Choose the most appropriate word from the box to complete the phrases. Change the word form if necessary.*

1. • _____ a lifelong goal
   • _____ great success
   • _____ desired results

2. • learn about the _____ of smoking
   • reduce the _____ of having a natural disaster
   • increase the _____ of accidents

3. • be absolutely _____
   • evacuate to a _____ place
   • provide _____ drinking water

4. • do a lot of _____
   • cause serious _____ to human health
   • prevent _____ from flooding

5. • exhibit _____ behavior
   • have an _____ personality
   • take _____ action against discrimination

> safe   aggressive   achieve   damage   risk

B *Choose the most appropriate word to complete the sentences.*

1. Judy likes to do _____ activities such as skydiving.
   a. job-seeking
   b. fame-seeking
   c. money-seeking
   d. thrill-seeking

2. If you win the lottery, it's going to be a _____ experience.
   a. day-in-day-out
   b. once-in-a-lifetime
   c. state-of-the-art
   d. top-of-the-line

Listening Comprehension WEB動画 🖥 📀DVD 🎧CD 1-37

A *Watch the video and choose the correct answers to the following questions.*

1. Stig is a freediver. In other words, _____.
   a. he dives only in his free time
   b. he dives just for fun
   c. he doesn't dive with an oxygen tank
   d. he doesn't dive with any other people

2. What does Sanna do?
   a. She is a teacher.
   b. She is a diver.
   c. She is a researcher.
   d. She is a swimmer.

3. In the areas Stig visits, _____.

    a. there are no reports of killer whales eating any marine mammals

    b. there are some sea creatures that eat killer whales

    c. there are many problems caused by marine pollution

    d. there are only a few people who enjoy surfing

B *Answer the following questions.*

1. In which country was this video filmed?

_____

2. Why does Stig visit Sanna before getting in the water?

_____

Tips on Listening and Speaking   1-39

Strong Forms / Weak Forms
Some words have both strong and weak forms. When a word is not very meaningful in a sentence, the pronunciation of the word often becomes weak. Here is an example of the word "that."

    1. Do you know who <u>that</u> man is?
                This "that" is pronounced in its strong form. [ðæt]
    2. It's important to think <u>that</u> everyone has different perspectives.
                This "that" is pronounced in its weak form. [ðət]

Dictation   1-40

Listen to the sentences and fill in the blanks.

1. He's here _____. Killer whales.

2. We have to _____.

3. We have clear blue skies and I have a feeling that
    I'm going to _____.

65

Retelling 　WEB動画 💻 📀 DVD

Watch the video again and tell the story of each scene to your partner. You can use the keywords given next to each picture.

e.g.

When Stig met Sanna

Keywords

dive, local inhabitants, get close to

Model

Stig went to Norway to dive with the local inhabitants, killer whales. Before diving, he asked Sanna about the risks of getting close to the animals.

1.

About Norwegian killer whales

Keywords

man-eater, damage, throw

2.

When Stig finally realized his dream

Keywords

pass by, playful, closest encounter

Discussion

Q: *Do you want to try swimming with whales in the sea? Why? Discuss your ideas with your partner.*

Your ideas	Your partner's ideas

Grammar

Noun Phrases Postmodified by Present Participles

Present participles can be used to add some more information to noun phrases.

That girl is my sister.
That girl <u>running over there</u> is my sister.
> *The speaker can express that the girl is running over there.*

The woman smiled brightly.
The woman <u>holding a bouquet of flowers</u> smiled brightly.
> *The speaker can express that the woman was holding a bouquet of flowers.*

The artist painted a beautiful scene of the river.
The artist painted a beautiful scene of the river <u>flowing gently through the valley</u>.
> *The speaker can express that the river was flowing gently through the valley.*

Grammar Exercise

Unscramble the following words and complete the sentences.

1. There were (a few / about / the flight / passengers / the delay / of / complaining).

   _____

2. (studying / people / two languages / number / more than / the / of) is increasing.

   _____

3. The doctor always makes every effort to save (patients / of / the lives / intractable diseases / suffering from).

   _____

4. (participated in / economics / the student / a study abroad program / majoring in) to learn about global economic systems.

   _____

5. Do you know (of / talking / with / the professor / the name) Jason?

   _____

6. (nuclear weapons / the abolition / for / of / fighting / the organization) plays an important role for world peace.

   _____

Reading

🎧 CD 1-41

There are a number of pressing issues pertaining to the ocean, such as rising sea levels, marine pollution, and the increasing number of endangered marine species. We should take these issues more seriously and attempt to achieve coexistence between human
5 beings and the ocean. In recent years, global recognition of the importance of "ocean education" has been steadily growing.

During the 2015 United Nations Summit, an agenda entitled "Transforming Our World: the 2030 Agenda for Sustainable Development" was announced. Of a total of 17 sub-goals, the 14th
10 is to conserve the richness of the oceans. UNESCO refers to the knowledge necessary for the achievement of coexistence between human beings and the ocean as "ocean literacy." This consists of seven fundamental principles. For example, the fourth principle states that the ocean plays a significant role in making the Earth
15 habitable, while the sixth principle emphasizes the inextricable nature of the connection between humans and the ocean.

Countries around the world have started to pay much more attention to ocean education to cultivate ocean literacy among children, and Japan is no exception. On Marine Day in 2016, the
20 Japanese government declared its aim to realize the implementation of ocean education by 2025 in all the wards, cities, towns, and villages across the country. This is especially important for Japan, which is surrounded by sea.

How should ocean education be conducted? Merely
25 acquiring knowledge about the oceans in a classroom is not sufficient. Experiencing various types of activities in the ocean firsthand is also of great importance. Real-life interactions with nature offer invaluable learning opportunities that cannot be replaced with what students learn from textbooks.

30 Human beings cannot live without nature. This is especially true of the ocean, which serves as a vital source of food, water, and energy. For future generations, it might be truly important to conduct ocean education to make children more aware of the importance of the ocean and feel stronger connections with it.
35 Cultivating people with such awareness is the initial step to conserving the ocean.

Vocabulary Check

Fill in the blanks with the words given in the box. Change the word form if necessary.

1. The _____ need for clean drinking water in this region is not recognized by the government.

2. The organization has taken various measures to protect _____ animals.

3. Access to educational resources plays a vital role in fostering _____ development.

4. Good communication skills are _____ to effective teamwork.

5. The Internet has become an _____ part of our daily lives.

> literacy   fundamental   pressing   endangered   inextricable

Reading Comprehension

Answer the following questions.

1. What are some of the ocean-related issues mentioned in the passage?

   _____

2. How does UNESCO define ocean literacy?

   _____

3. What goal did the Japanese government announce in 2016?

   _____

4. In addition to acquiring relevant knowledge, what is important in the practice of ocean education?

   _____

UNIT 1 UNIT 2 UNIT 3 UNIT 4 UNIT 5 UNIT 6 UNIT 7 UNIT 8 UNIT 9 UNIT 10 UNIT 11 UNIT 12 UNIT 13 UNIT 14 UNIT 15

Writing

A *Write a proposal for an ocean education program in 70-80 words, considering the following points.*

❏ What activities are included in the program?
❏ Which school grade is the target of the program?
❏ What skills are students expected to develop through the program?

Useful Expressions

The program includes a variety of activities to …
The program targets … students.
The target population of the program is …
By participating in the program, students will gain …
The program aims to equip students with the skill to …

Useful Vocabulary

experience snorkeling   observe fishing activities   conduct fieldwork in the ocean
investigate the main cause of marine litter   think about sustainable use of marine resources

B *Make pairs and share your ideas with your partner. Write down what your partner has shared with you.*

How to Become a Standout Footballer

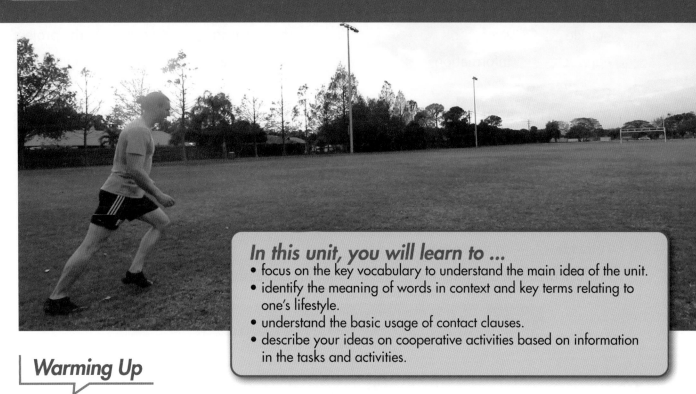

In this unit, you will learn to ...
- focus on the key vocabulary to understand the main idea of the unit.
- identify the meaning of words in context and key terms relating to one's lifestyle.
- understand the basic usage of contact clauses.
- describe your ideas on cooperative activities based on information in the tasks and activities.

Warming Up

Choose or write your own answers to the following questions. Then ask your partner the questions.

1. What sport did you play when you were in senior high school?
   - ❏ None
   - ❏ Baseball
   - ❏ Soccer
   - ❏ Other ( )

2. How often do you play sports?
   - ❏ Almost every day
   - ❏ Once a month
   - ❏ Once a week
   - ❏ Other ( )

3. Which do you prefer, playing sports yourself or watching sports? Why?

_____

Watching

WEB動画 🖥️ 💿 DVD 💿 CD 2-01

Watch the video and write a brief outline in approximately five sentences.

Vocabulary 🔊 CD 2-02

A *Choose the most appropriate word from the box to complete the phrases. Change the word form if necessary.*

1. • be _____ to other people's feelings
   • tackle _____ issues
   • protect _____ information

2. • lack _____
   • show strong _____ to complete the project
   • make a final _____ to study abroad

3. • _____ to figure out the theory
   • _____ for educational equality
   • _____ against discrimination

4. • understand my own _____ and weaknesses
   • develop mental _____
   • increase physical _____

5. • need a lot of _____ and direction
   • provide _____ to the student
   • write a dissertation under the _____ of a famous professor

> sensitive   determination   strength   struggle   guidance

B *Choose the most appropriate phrase to complete the sentences.*

1. I was very nervous during the job interview. I _____ my answers and didn't get the job.
   a. boosted up
   b. cheered up
   c. messed up
   d. fixed up

2. It's important to _____ between work and life to stay healthy.
   a. balance the scales
   b. take the risks
   c. acknowledge the importance
   d. complicate the situation

Listening Comprehension 💻WEB動画 📀DVD 🔊CD 2-01

A *Watch the video and choose the correct answers to the following questions.*

1. At what age, was Spencer a sensitive and shy player?
   a. 11-12
   b. 13-14
   c. 15-16
   d. 17-18

2. Spencer found a mentor who helped him _____.
   a. develop his technical skills
   b. master his mind
   c. become sensitive to his teammates' feelings
   d. increase his physical strength

3. In order to improve his performance on the pitch, Spencer _____.

    a. found a new hobby

    b. attempted to have more sleep

    c. changed the method of training

    d. got out of his comfort zone

B *Answer the following questions.*

1. How long has Spencer been playing football?

    _____

2. What does Spencer think is the greatest question to ask?

    _____

Tips on Listening and Speaking   🎧 2-03

Agreement Expressions with Inversion

Some expressions used to show agreement have non-standard word order.

    A: I'm very busy these days.
    B: <u>So am I</u>. When can we be free?

    C: My daughter went to Australia to study English last year.
    D: <u>So did my son</u>! Where in Australia did she go?

Dictation   🎧 2-04

Listen to the sentences and fill in the blanks.

1. _____, was to become a professional football player.

2. When your dream is to kick a ball around a grass field for ninety minutes _____ _____ and perform a quality touch, you realize something needs to change.

3. As my mental strength grew, _____.

Retelling

Watch the video again and tell the story of each scene to your partner. You can use the keywords given next to each picture.

e.g.

The reason why Spencer made this video

Keywords

share, tip, pitch

Model

Spencer is a vlogger and footballer from the U.S. He made this video to share some of the best tips he learned over his career. By doing so, he hoped to help watchers become good players and even better people off the pitch.

1.

When Spencer was younger

Keywords

determination, poor performance, technique

2.

The way Spencer changed himself

Keywords

admit, self-confidence, positivity

Discussion

Q: *What was your dream when you were younger? Is it still the same now? Discuss your ideas with your partner.*

Your ideas	Your partner's ideas

74

Grammar

(Contact Clause)

When object relative clauses are used to modify nouns, relative pronouns can be omitted. This type of relative clause without a relative pronoun is called a contact clause. Contact clauses are often used in everyday conversation to simplify sentences. On the other hand, in formal writing, it is considered better to keep the relative pronoun for clarity.

The bag that Lisa bought yesterday is expensive.
The bag Lisa bought yesterday is expensive.
The relative pronoun "that" is omitted.

The actor whom I saw near Shibuya Station looked very tired.
The actor I saw near Shibuya Station looked very tired.
The relative pronoun "whom" is omitted.

Grammar Exercise

Unscramble the following words and complete the sentences.

1. The (used / Katherine / a long time / computer / for / is / has) about to break.

   _____

2. The nurse is still (the doctor / yesterday / about / examined / the patient / worried).

   _____

3. Yuta is (respect / basketball / of / players / I / one / the).

   _____

4. The (meeting / boss / made / suggestion / the / during / my) was not supported by the participants.

   _____

5. Mike utilized (obtained / knowledge / intern / a lot of / when / he / from / his) he started his business.

   _____

6. The (John / last week / difficult / plan / proposed / seemed) to carry out.

   _____

It is widely accepted that starting one's professional career as early as possible is key to achieving success in the world of professional sports. One rationale for this viewpoint is that athletes have more time to develop their skills and gain experience, which probably leads to a longer and more 5 successful career. However, there are always exceptions to this notion, and one of the most prominent examples is Kaoru Mitoma, a Japanese football player.

Mitoma was born in 1997 and began his football career by joining the academy of his local J-League team, Kawasaki Frontale, at the age of 10 nine. When he was 18 years old, he was offered a professional contract by Kawasaki's senior team, but he decided not to sign it. Instead, he enrolled in University of Tsukuba, where he majored in sports science while continuing to play football for the university's team.

One of the main reasons for his decision is that he thought he was not 15 ready to play in the professional world. He felt that he needed more time to prepare to become a player who could compete with other professionals. In order to become a better player, Mitoma learned many things at university. The most outstanding thing is that for his bachelor's thesis, he conducted research on the difference between good and not-so-good dribblers. By 20 asking participants in his study to wear a camera on their forehead, he recorded their behavior as they played. This experience arguably had a positive impact on his later career.

In 2020, he made his professional debut. In his first J-League season, he performed brilliantly, recording 13 goals and 12 assists in 30 matches. He 25 played in the Tokyo Olympics in 2021 as well as the FIFA World Cup in 2022. In the match against Spain in the World Cup, Mitoma provided an assist for a teammate's goal by tenaciously pursuing a ball that had nearly crossed the goal line. This feat, which is known as "Mitoma's one millimeter," made him even more famous all over the world.

30 Following accepted notions is not always the right thing to do. What seems to be more important is to analyze yourself and find out what is most appropriate for you. Mitoma is a successful example of this. He made his own decision about the best time to turn professional by thinking deeply about what was best for himself.

Vocabulary Check

Fill in the blanks with the words given in the box. Change the word form if necessary.

1. In our team, every member is required attend the weekly meeting, without _____.
2. Some people do not agree with the traditional _____ of family.
3. _____ with stronger players may help you improve your technical skills.
4. The _____ performance of the actor in the movie moved many people.
5. John is still not sure what job is most _____ for him.

> exception   suitable   compete   outstanding   notion

Reading Comprehension

Answer the following questions.

1. Why do many people think it is better to start one's professional career early?

   _____

2. What happened to Mitoma when he was 18 years old?

   _____

3. What did Mitoma do for his bachelor's thesis?

   _____

4. What made Mitoma even more famous in the world?

   _____

77

Writing

A *Write about yourself in an objective manner in 70-80 words, considering the following points.*

❑ What are your strengths?

❑ What are your weaknesses?

❑ What do you think is needed to overcome your weaknesses?

B *Make pairs and share your ideas with your partner. Write down what your partner has shared with you.*

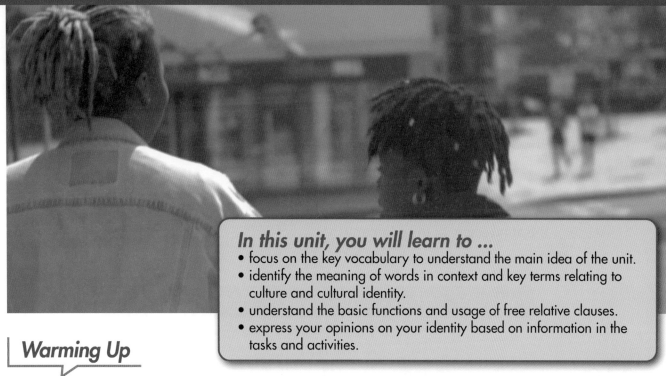

In this unit, you will learn to ...
- focus on the key vocabulary to understand the main idea of the unit.
- identify the meaning of words in context and key terms relating to culture and cultural identity.
- understand the basic functions and usage of free relative clauses.
- express your opinions on your identity based on information in the tasks and activities.

Warming Up

Choose or write your own answers to the following questions. Then ask your partner the questions.

1. How often do you have your hair cut?
   - ❏ Once a month
   - ❏ Once every two months
   - ❏ Once every three months
   - ❏ Other ( )

2. How much do you spend on fashion-related items each month?
   - ❏ Less than 5,000 yen
   - ❏ 5,000-20,000 yen
   - ❏ More than 20,000 yen
   - ❏ Other ( )

3. Do you like to change your hairstyle frequently? Why?

_____

Watching

WEB動画 DVD CD 2-06

Watch the video and write a brief outline in approximately five sentences.

Vocabulary 🎧 2-07

A *Choose the most appropriate word from the box to complete the phrases. Change the word form if necessary.*

1. • make a _____
   • provide a _____
   • issue a _____

2. • _____ the quality
   • _____ close contact with my friend
   • _____ that learning about global issues is important

3. • professional _____
   • cultural _____
   • personal _____

4. • _____ viewpoints
   • _____ image of the culture
   • _____ gender roles

5. • _____ diversity
   • _____ the anniversary of the company
   • _____ the launch of the new product

> maintain   statement   stereotypical   identity   celebrate

B *Choose the most appropriate meaning of the underlined expressions.*

1. The book cover with an intricate geometric design makes it <u>eye-catching</u> on the bookstore shelf.

   a. tedious
   b. attractive
   c. unremarkable
   d. ordinary

2. The financial hardships and obstacles in his career did not <u>deter</u> Mike from starting his own business.

   a. enable
   b. promote
   c. discourage
   d. assist

Listening Comprehension 💻WEB動画 📀DVD 🎧CD 2-06

A *Watch the video and choose the correct answers to the following questions.*

1. Marc Hare is a _____.

   a. shoe designer
   b. fashion model
   c. hair stylist
   d. taxi driver

2. Dreadlocks have been recognized as part of London's _____ identity.

   a. personal
   b. regional
   c. political
   d. visual

3. Why does Marc wear dreadlocks?

   a. To be popular among his customers.

   b. To let people know he is rich.

   c. To show pride in his culture.

   d. To express his feelings.

B *Answer the following questions.*

1. Where can you find dreadlocks in London? Pick up three examples from the video.

_____

2. How does the importance of cultural identity make Marc feel?

_____

Tips on Listening and Speaking 2-08

Special Connotation

Even simple words can take on a special connotation when used in an idiom. In such cases, it is important to be cautious in interpretation because the meaning may no longer make sense based on its commonly used connotation.

   1. I'll be happy to plan the party, but you'll need to <u>foot the bill</u> for the venue and catering.
   2. As the director, it's your responsibility to make all the major decisions and <u>run the show</u>.

Dictation 2-09

Listen to the sentences and fill in the blanks.

1. Wherever you go in London, there are _____.

2. They're proud of _____.

3. They mean a lot to _____.

Retelling WEB動画 🖥 💿DVD

Watch the video again and tell the story of each scene to your partner. You can use the keywords given next to each picture.

e.g.

About London dreadlocks

Keywords

style, maintain, unique

Model

There are some people who wear dreadlocks in London. Dreadlocks are a way of styling your hair. There are many types of unique dreadlocks, but you need to make a lot of effort to maintain them.

1.

About Marc Hare

Keywords

run, designer, with pride

2.

How important dreadlocks are to Marc

Keywords

self-expression, professional, cultural

Discussion

Q: *In your society, are there any stereotypical views on people? Discuss your ideas with your partner.*

Your ideas	Your partner's ideas

Grammar

(**Free Relative Clause**)

Standard relative clauses are used to modify a noun phrase. On the other hand, when free relative clauses are used, there is no overt antecedent. Rather, free relative clauses themselves act as a noun phrase.

<u>What she said</u> made him sad.
"What she said" is the subject of this sentence. The speaker can express that she said something, and it made him sad.

Grammar Exercise

Unscramble the following words and complete the sentences.

1. (for / we / what / to / the environment / need / do) is to reduce the amount of garbage.

   _____

2. (wants / her birthday / what / Mary / for) is a new smartphone.

   _____

3. (important / health / is / maintain / good / what / to) is having well-balanced meals.

   _____

4. (to / is / necessary / what / a good researcher / become) is curiosity about everything.

   _____

5. (you / to / what / emphasize / during / want / the presentation) should be highlighted so that the audience can understand it clearly.

   _____

6. (weekend / you / to / what / last / said / Ben) seemed to make him sad.

   _____

CD 2-10

Identity is a multifaceted concept that defines who we are as individuals and how we relate to the world around us. Self-identity is deeply personal and can profoundly affect our self-esteem. In recent times, among various facets of self-identity, the diversity of gender identity has attracted considerable attention among English speakers, which is reflected in their language usage.

5   You have probably learned that the following sentence is not grammatically correct: *Charlie is my best friend, and I often go shopping with them*. Since *Charlie* is third person singular, using *her* or *him* may be more natural. However, do you know that this sentence can be grammatically correct depending on the situation where it is used? This pertains closely to the growing recognition of various types of gender identity.

10   In English, there are three different types of third-person pronouns: *he*, *she*, and *they*. Traditionally, the pronouns *he*, *she,* and *they* are used to refer to a male person, a female person, and multiple people, respectively. You may choose a pronoun to refer to a certain person based on the person's biological gender, but there can be a mismatch between the person's gender and the pronoun you use to refer to the person.

15   Some people do not feel comfortable with the traditional gender binary concept of "either male or female," because this strict distinction can lead to imposing specific gender roles on individuals. Recently, English speakers have developed a new standard that allows them to decide their own personal pronouns. For example, you have probably found that some English-speaking people add their preferred pronoun(s) to their social media profile, like "she/her" or "he/him," for 20 example.

You may also find some people adding "they/them" in their profile. This means that they recognize themselves as non-binary, indicating that they prefer not to categorize themselves as strictly male or female. When referring to these people, it is appropriate to use *they*, rather than *he* or *she*. Returning to the example sentence in the second paragraph, you can now understand why 25 it is not grammatically incorrect in certain contexts. The choice of pronouns is important because they are often used in daily conversation. Misgendering someone, even if it is unintentional, can be hurtful.

Gender identity is a component that comprises our self-identity. Using "they" as a third-person singular pronoun is becoming the new normal. As an English user in today's world, where 30 diversity is being embraced, understanding how pronouns matter in English may be of great significance.

84

Vocabulary Check

Fill in the blanks with the words given in the box. Change the word form if necessary.

1. More and more people have come to _____ cultural diversity.

2. Some experts propose that it is necessary to _____ stricter penalties for certain crimes.

3. Genetic factors have a significant influence on the determination of an individual's _____ characteristics.

4. When you make _____ mistakes, trying to learn something from them is crucial.

5. The research team _____ five professionals from various backgrounds.

| biological | impose | embrace | comprise | unintentional |

Reading Comprehension

Answer the following questions.

1. How are pronouns traditionally chosen to refer to someone?

_____

2. Why do some people feel uncomfortable with a gender binary?

_____

3. If some people add "they/them" to their profile, what does that mean?

_____

4. Why is the choice of pronouns important in English?

_____

Writing

A *Write about your opinion of self-expression in 70-80 words, considering the following points.*

❏ Are you always free to express yourself without restrictions?
❏ In what ways do you like to express yourself?
❏ What significance does self-expression have for you?

B *Make pairs and share your ideas with your partner. Write down what your partner has shared with you.*

UNIT 11 Earthships

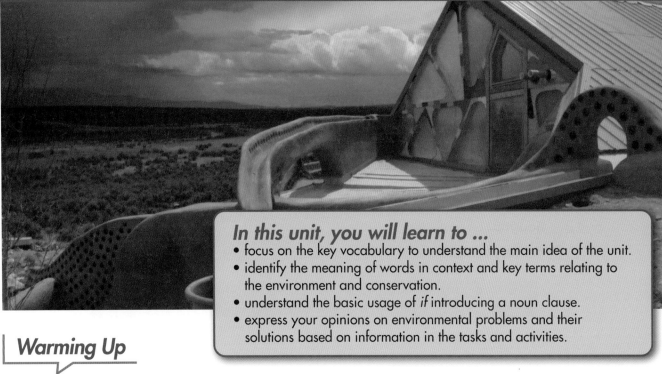

In this unit, you will learn to ...
- focus on the key vocabulary to understand the main idea of the unit.
- identify the meaning of words in context and key terms relating to the environment and conservation.
- understand the basic usage of *if* introducing a noun clause.
- express your opinions on environmental problems and their solutions based on information in the tasks and activities.

Warming Up

Choose or write your own answers to the following questions. Then ask your partner the questions.

1. What environmental conservation practices do you usually engage in?
   - ❑ Water conservation
   - ❑ Waste separation
   - ❑ Use of reusable bags
   - ❑ Other ( )

2. What changes have you noticed in your local area as a result of climate change?
   - ❑ Frequent flooding
   - ❑ Decreased snowfall in winter
   - ❑ Frequent heatwaves in summer
   - ❑ Other ( )

3. What do you think is the most serious environmental issue at present? And why?

_____

Watching
WEB動画 DVD CD 2-11

Watch the video and write a brief outline in approximately five sentences.

Vocabulary 🎧 2-12

A *Choose the most appropriate word from the box to complete the phrases. Change the word form if necessary.*

1. • _____ ultraviolet rays
   • _____ heat and cold
   • _____ new knowledge

2. • a _____ development
   • design a _____ house
   • be improved by the _____ software

3. • _____ rainwater
   • _____ fresh vegetables for dinner
   • _____ wind power

4. • the utilization of the _____
   • an incidental _____
   • be obtained as a _____

5. • _____ learners
   • _____ housing
   • _____ delivery vehicles

> harvest   autonomous   absorb   by-product   revolutionary

B *Choose the most appropriate meaning of the underlined expressions.*

1. During the holiday season, the shopping mall becomes a <u>hive of activity</u>.

   a. busy place
   b. sorrowful place
   c. sophisticated place
   d. beautiful place

2. She helped others, <u>regardless of</u> their social status.

   a. as well as
   b. judging from
   c. based on
   d. without considering

Listening Comprehension   WEB動画 💻 DVD 🎧 2-11

A *Watch the video and choose the correct answers to the following questions.*

1. Where are Earthships located?

   a. In the mountains
   b. In the desert
   c. In the ocean
   d. In the urban areas

2. What is Michael Reynolds's role?

   a. A lead instructor at the Earthship Academy
   b. A famous journalist reporting on sustainable housing projects
   c. A skilled engineer of renewable energy systems
   d. A visionary architect who has improved sustainable housing techniques

3. Earthships could be the answer to some of our future problems, _____.

    a. as climate change is forcing us to question the way we live

    b. although government policies and regulations are limiting them

    c. since they are more attractive than housing in space

    d. but they are too expensive to build and maintain

B *Answer the following questions.*

1. How are the walls of Earthships constructed?

    _____

2. How does the environment inside the Earthships differ from the outside?

    _____

Tips on Listening and Speaking 2-13

Sentence Stress

Speakers may emphasize certain words or phrases. The stressed parts can provide important information.

    A: What language have you been studying?
    B: I've been studying <u>French</u> for three years.

    C: How long have you been studying a foreign language?
    D: I've been studying French for <u>three years</u>.

Dictation 2-14

Listen to the sentences and fill in the blanks.

1. The walls of the Earthships are built with car tires tightly packed with dirt and

    _____.

2. The tires are _____ like it does.

3. In the early 70s, the news was talking about _____

    and highway, cans and bottles.

Retelling

Watch the video again and tell the story of each scene to your partner. You can use the keywords given next to each picture.

e.g.

About Earthship Academy

Keywords

students,   off-the-grid,   housing

Model

The purpose of Earthship Academy is to teach students from all over the world about building sustainable houses. The Earthship Academy has 33 students. They learn how to build sustainable, off-the-grid, autonomous housing there.

1.

About the Earthship

Keywords

a mini-biosphere,   an Amazon jungle, nuclear power plants

2.

The building in the Earthship

Keywords

a bucket-flush toilet,   a solar-bag shower, your cell phone

Discussion

Q: *Would you like to stay in an Earthship? Why? Discuss your ideas with your partner.*

Your ideas	Your partner's ideas

Grammar

"If" Introducing a Noun Clause

Besides forming an adverbial clause expressing a condition, "if" also serves the function of introducing a noun clause that expresses the meaning of whether. In this context, we can use "whether" instead of "if."

I don't know **if (or whether) he will come**.

However, if the clause functions as the subject or complement, "if" should not be used; in such instances, employ "whether."
- **Whether Noah can receive a scholarship** depends on his grades this semester.
- The problem is **whether the airplane will arrive on schedule.**

Grammar Exercise

Unscramble the following words and complete the sentences.

1. We will need to check the weather forecast to see (rain / before / will / planning / if / it / tomorrow) our outdoor activities.

   _____

2. The team is (complete / if / discussing / possible / it's / to) the project by the deadline.

   _____

3. It's unclear (new / whether/ will / brand / launch / a / the company) this year.

   _____

4. (product / the / customer / expectations / whether / meets) is a crucial factor in its success.

   _____

5. I'm not (the / effectively / if / will / sure / economic / reforms) address the underlying issues facing the nation.

   _____

6. The critical factor is (performance / whether / can / maintain / consistent / the players).

   _____

Reading

🔊 2-15

Although "recycling" has now become a widely used word, the term "upcycling" may not be so familiar. Both upcycling and recycling are significant concepts for sustainable resource management, but they differ in their approaches.

5 Recycling involves collecting and reprocessing waste or used materials to create new products. For instance, plastic bottles can be collected, transformed into recycled plastic, and used to produce new plastic items. Recycling cuts waste and minimizes the need for new raw materials, thereby reducing the environmental impact of production. On the other hand, upcycling focuses on reusing used materials to add value or functionality. It promotes resource conservation and 10 waste reduction through repurposing. For example, old jeans can be transformed into backpacks, and used wood can be repurposed to create tables or furniture.

To take another example, recycling plastic bottles involves collecting, sorting, and reprocessing them to manufacture new plastic products. Meanwhile, upcycling explores innovative uses, such as turning them into vases or lampshades, while retaining their original form and 15 characteristics. Upcycling can be seen as a sustainable alternative to traditional recycling because it requires fewer resources and less energy to transform items into something new. It promotes environmental consciousness and reduces the demand for new materials, thus contributing to a more sustainable and circular economy.

As in many other countries worldwide, the upcycling movement is also growing in Japan. 20 An interesting project has started in Tokyo, where a sandwich shop and a coffee shop are teaming up with a beer company. They are making unique beers using leftover ingredients that would otherwise be thrown away. The sandwich shop uses bread crusts to create a wheat beer, and while the coffee shop repurposes test-roasted coffee beans for a dark beer. This upcycling movement has inspired many local businesses to collaborate, making the local community more active than 25 before.

Are there any upcycling projects in your local area as well? Achieving large-scale projects like Earthships may take time, but you may be able to start with a small upcycling attempt in your daily life. Why not start enjoying a sustainable life?

Vocabulary Check

Fill in the blanks with the words given in the box. Change the word form if necessary.

1. To _____ the risk of infection, wash your hands frequently and avoid touching your face.
2. The pizza had a thin and crispy _____.
3. The old factory was _____ into a trendy art gallery.
4. The website's search _____ allows users to quickly find related information.
5. The secret _____ in this sauce is a spoonful of blue cheese.

| minimize functionality repurpose ingredient crust |

Reading Comprehension

Answer the following questions.

1. What does recycling involve?

   _____

2. What is an example of an upcycling project using old jeans?

   _____

3. Why can upcycling be seen as a sustainable alternative to traditional recycling?

   _____

4. What is an example of an upcycling project in Tokyo?

   _____

Writing

A *Create your own upcycling project, and write about it in 70-80 words, considering the following points.*

❏ What kind of waste or used materials would you like to upcycle?

❏ What would you like to create through upcycling?

❏ What kind of impact would your upcycling efforts have on the environment and society?

Useful Expressions

It would be effective to repurpose …
It is a problem that … is being discarded.
By creating … from …, we can …
By not wasting …, we can …
… would be a creative and eco-friendly product.

Useful Vocabulary

reinvent discarded materials   provide a sustainable alternative   redesign clothes
redevelop a product   have a positive influence on the environment

B *Make pairs and share your ideas with your partner. Write down what your partner has shared with you.*

Fill My Tank

In this unit, you will learn to ...
- focus on the key vocabulary to understand the main idea of the unit.
- identify the meaning of words in context and key terms relating to biotechnology.
- understand the basic functions and usage of comparative expressions.
- express your opinions on clean energy based on information in the tasks and activities.

Warming Up

Choose or write your own answers to the following questions. Then ask your partner the questions.

1. What is one reason why you would travel?
   - ❏ To learn about different cultures
   - ❏ To escape from everyday life
   - ❏ To enjoy local cuisine
   - ❏ Other (   )

2. Which of the following clean energy sources have you heard of?
   - ❏ Biomass
   - ❏ Hydroelectric power
   - ❏ Tidal power
   - ❏ Other (   )

3. Due to environmental considerations, the use of reusable bags is recommended. Which do you usually use, a reusable bag or a plastic bag? Why?

_____

Watching

WEB動画 🖥️ 📀 DVD 📀 CD 2-16

Watch the video and write a brief outline in approximately five sentences.

Vocabulary
🎧 2-17

A *Choose the most appropriate word from the box to complete the phrases. Change the word form if necessary.*

1. • _____ a document into PDF format
   • _____ analog audio to digital
   • _____ a room into a home office

2. • alternatives to _____
   • _____ consumption
   • _____ emissions

3. • environmental _____
   • water _____
   • noise _____

4. • meet a _____ for lunch
   • many _____ from different departments
   • support by some _____

5. • _____ design
   • _____ technologies
   • _____ heating and cooling systems

| energy-efficient   convert   fossil fuel   pollution   colleague |

B *Choose the most appropriate meaning of the underlined expressions.*

1. The problem was solved by our manager <u>in no time</u>.
   a. under the weather
   b. at any cost
   c. in doubt
   d. very quickly

2. It's time to say goodbye and <u>get going</u> on our individual journeys.
   a. save face
   b. make a start
   c. run in circles
   d. go hand in hand

Listening Comprehension
WEB動画 🖥 📀 DVD 🎧 CD 2-16

A *Watch the video and choose the correct answers to the following questions.*

1. Where is the factory located that can produce fuel in a revolutionary way?
   a. Cambodia
   b. Singapore
   c. Colombia
   d. Zambia

2. In the video, biofuels are described as _____.
   a. renewable sources like plants
   b. fossil fuels like coal
   c. synthetic metals
   d. organic substances like animal waste

3. What will Sean do with the converter?

    a. Donate it to a different orphanage.

    b. Keep it as a personal souvenir.

    c. Use it to power his camera equipment.

    d. Use it to fuel his car's journey to the orphanage.

B *Answer the following questions.*

1. What does Sean need to get first before visiting the orphanage?

_____

2. Why has the crowd gathered in the orphanage?

_____

Tips on Listening and Speaking   🎧 2-18

Metaphorical Expressions

In everyday conversation, metaphorical expressions are used to convey a subtle nuance effectively. These expressions often have non-literal meanings, so we should be careful both in understanding and using them.

    1. Example of a literal meaning
       The bartender **broke the ice** into small pieces and put them in the wine cooler.
    2. Example of a non-literal meaning
       In the first lecture, the professor organized a game to help the students **break the ice** and get to know each other.

In the second example sentence, "break the ice" refers to saying or doing something to make people who have not met before feel relaxed with each other.

Dictation   🎧 2-19

Listen to the sentences and fill in the blanks.

1. _____. Is this the coffee machine?

2. _____, and Sean demonstrates how it works.

3. All the steps are here for you to follow later on, _____
    properly.

UNIT 1
UNIT 2
UNIT 3
UNIT 4
UNIT 5
UNIT 6
UNIT 7
UNIT 8
UNIT 9
UNIT 10
UNIT 11
UNIT 12
UNIT 13
UNIT 14
UNIT 15

Retelling

Watch the video again and tell the story of each scene to your partner. You can use the keywords given next to each picture.

e.g.

About Sean Lee Davis

Keywords

photographer,   travel,   green technology

Model

Sean is a writer, photographer, and filmmaker. He travels the world covering green issues and green technology.

1.

About a green orphanage

Keywords

Sunrise,   be known for,   technology

2.

Differences between biofuels and fossil fuels

Keywords

easier to make,   greener,   coal

Discussion

Q: If you were to participate in a biofuelled trip mentioned in the video, which role would you like to play? Would you deliver converters to a place 2,500 km away or develop converters? Would you like to do both? And why? Discuss your ideas with your partner.

Your ideas	Your partner's ideas

Grammar

Comparative Expressions

There are three forms of comparative expressions in English.

Comparative degree: Used when comparing two things.
- Mary is **taller than** her sister.
- This book is **more interesting than** any other book I've read.

Superlative degree: Used when comparing three or more things.
- Mount Everest is **the highest** mountain in the world.
- Sam is **the most talented** musician in the group.

Positive degree: Used to indicate equality between two things.
- The new restaurant is **as popular as** the one we visited last month.

Grammar Exercise

Unscramble the following words and complete the sentences.

1. William (the / receiving / promotion / felt / after / happier), but he realized that money alone couldn't make him truly satisfied.

   _____

2. (most / is / one / of / the / breathtaking / the Grand Canyon) natural wonders in the world.

   _____

3. The film proved to (had / as / be / exciting / anticipated / as / I).

   _____

4. The hotel we stayed (one / was / than / nicer / the / at last year) we are in now.

   _____

5. The marathon runner (the / time / finished / the race / shortest / in).

   _____

6. This new smartphone is (model / the / powerful / as / latest / as) but more affordable.

   _____

UNIT 1 UNIT 2 UNIT 3 UNIT 4 UNIT 5 UNIT 6 UNIT 7 UNIT 8 UNIT 9 UNIT 10 UNIT 11 UNIT 12 UNIT 13 UNIT 14 UNIT 15

2-20

Since the 1980s, when people became concerned about global warming, finding sustainable energy sources has become a major issue worldwide. Switching from fossil fuels to clean energy has been a significant challenge for humanity. Renewable
5 energy sources, such as wind energy, solar energy, biomass energy, and hydrogen energy, have been developed as alternatives to fossil fuels. Although there has been progress in their development, the use of clean energy is still not widespread.

There are several reasons why clean energy is not
10 spreading quickly. First, it is costly. Clean energy technologies and equipment can be more expensive compared to conventional fossil fuels, so it takes a lot of money to implement them. Second, there's a lack of infrastructure. The extensive utilization of clean energy requires the development of renewable energy power
15 plants and charging stations. Building such infrastructure takes both time and financial resources. Another issue is that many countries and regions depend on existing energy systems. Policies and profit-driven interests associated with fossil fuels can make it hard for clean energy to become common.

20 Furthermore, there might not be enough regulations and policies to encourage clean energy adoption. Without proper support from governments, businesses may be less willing to invest in clean energy. Lastly, there is a lack of information. When people and businesses do not have accurate and accessible
25 information about the benefits of clean energy, they may not fully understand its potential. A combination of these factors may slow the spread of clean energy. However, increased attention, technological advances, and improved policies may help promote its spread.

30 One indicator of clean energy penetration is the market share of electric vehicles (EVs). Recent reports on new car sales in Japan reveal that EVs make up only about 0.9% of total car sales. In contrast, the share of EVs in new car sales in the EU is approximately 9%. In Norway, the share is a remarkable 64.5%.
35 Moreover, China's electric vehicle market share is over 11%. Clean energy adoption in Japan still seems to be behind global standards. We need to explore measures that can accelerate its adoption. What would you suggest to overcome the energy problem?

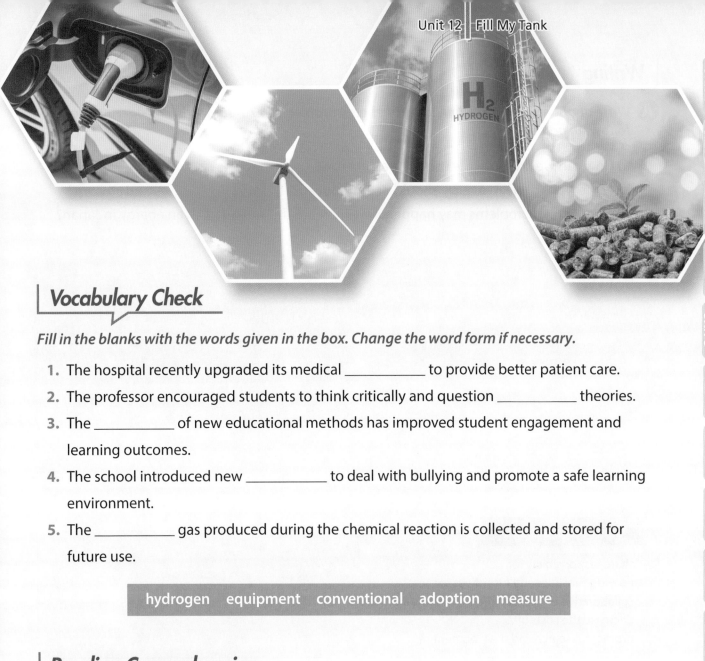

Vocabulary Check

Fill in the blanks with the words given in the box. Change the word form if necessary.

1. The hospital recently upgraded its medical _____ to provide better patient care.

2. The professor encouraged students to think critically and question _____ theories.

3. The _____ of new educational methods has improved student engagement and learning outcomes.

4. The school introduced new _____ to deal with bullying and promote a safe learning environment.

5. The _____ gas produced during the chemical reaction is collected and stored for future use.

> hydrogen   equipment   conventional   adoption   measure

Reading Comprehension

Answer the following questions.

1. What has been a major global concern since the 1980s?

   _____

2. What does the extensive utilization of clean energy require?

   _____

3. How does the lack of proper government regulation, policy, or other support affect businesses?

   _____

4. What percentage of Japan's new vehicle sales comprises electric vehicles?

   _____

Writing

Ⓐ *Write about a suggestion you have for energy problems in 70-80 words, considering the following points.*

❏ How can we promote the use of clean energy?

❏ What types of clean energy should be introduced?

❏ What kind of problems may happen if we increase the spread of clean energy in Japan?

Ⓑ *Make pairs and share your ideas with your partner. Write down what your partner has shared with you.*

How to Make Money and Travel Full Time

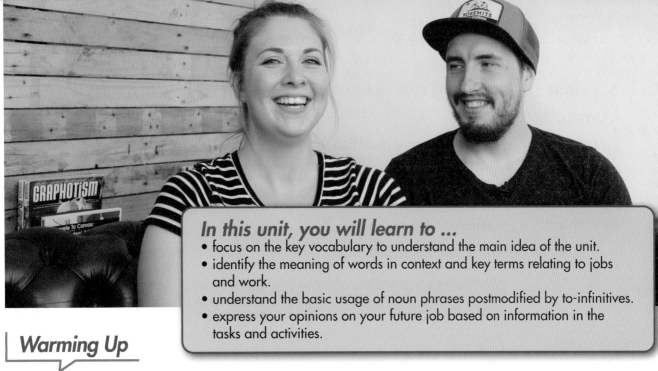

In this unit, you will learn to ...
- focus on the key vocabulary to understand the main idea of the unit.
- identify the meaning of words in context and key terms relating to jobs and work.
- understand the basic usage of noun phrases postmodified by to-infinitives.
- express your opinions on your future job based on information in the tasks and activities.

Warming Up

Choose or write your own answers to the following questions. Then ask your partner the questions.

1. How do you prefer to travel?
   - ❏ By car
   - ❏ By train
   - ❏ By ship
   - ❏ Other (   )

2. If you were to open an online shop, what would you sell?
   - ❏ Clothes
   - ❏ Accessories
   - ❏ Photographs
   - ❏ Other (   )

3. Which type of working style would you choose, working from a traditional office environment, working from home, or being a digital nomad (a remote worker who travels)? And why?

_____

Watching

WEB動画 🖥️ 📀 DVD 💿 CD 2-21

Watch the video and write a brief outline in approximately five sentences.

Vocabulary 🎧 2-22

A *Choose the most appropriate word from the box to complete the phrases. Change the word form if necessary.*

1. • a challenging and _____ career
   • _____ outcome
   • be _____ in achieving the goal

2. • have a job _____
   • arrange an in-person _____
   • during the _____

3. • a large _____ of clothing in various sizes
   • run out of _____
   • an excellent _____ of teaching materials

4. • main source of _____
   • have a high _____
   • earn an _____

5. • have a fantastic and _____ time at the festival
   • fun and _____ activities
   • _____ dinner conversations with family

income	successful	stock	interview	enjoyable

B *Choose the most appropriate phrase to complete the sentences.*

1. The college student got a part-time job to _____ for expenses.
   a. make money
   b. pay the check
   c. pay in cash
   d. create coins

2. _____ is a type of boat designed for navigating canals, primarily in the UK.
   a. A speedboat
   b. A steamboat
   c. A narrowboat
   d. A sailboat

Listening Comprehension WEB動画 📀 DVD 🎧 2-21

A *Watch the video and choose the correct answers to the following questions.*

1. Bee and Theo have been traveling _____.
   a. since 2010
   b. since 2012
   c. since 2014
   d. since 2016

2. What is the first thing they recommend creating to make money online?
   a. A YouTube channel
   b. A really nice looking website
   c. An online shop
   d. Social media accounts

3. How does Theo describe being able to make money doing something he loves?

   a. It's grateful.

   b. It's stressful.

   c. It's boring.

   d. It's brilliant.

B *Answer the following questions.*

1. There are many different ways to make money online. What are the three examples given by Bee and Theo as creative ways to do so?

   _____

2. Who did Bee and Theo want to interview?

   _____

Tips on Listening and Speaking   2-23

Expressions of Gratitude

Many conversations begin and end with expressing gratitude. There are various expressions of gratitude, and it is important to use them appropriately based on the situation and the relationship with the other person. For example, "grateful" is used to express gratitude to someone, often in the form "be grateful to someone/for something." In situations where you want to express gratitude more formally or politely, you can use "appreciate." However, it is important to note that "appreciate" refers to specific things or actions, not to your feeling toward another person.

   1. **Thank you for** the explanation.
   2. **I'm grateful to** my grandparents for their support.
   3. **I'm grateful for** your support.
   4. I **appreciate** the opportunity you have given me.
   5. I'd **appreciate** it if you could send me the information.

Dictation   2-24

Listen to the sentences and fill in the blanks.

1. _____ within two days.

2. It's really simple to do and _____.

3. _____ on the next video.

Retelling

Watch the video again and tell the story of each scene to your partner. You can use the keywords given next to each picture.

e.g.

About transportation and important things for Bee and Theo's travels

> **Keywords**
>
> a narrowboat, successful, happy

Model

They travel in a camper van and a narrowboat. They feel that working from where you are happy is important for being successful.

1. THE INDIE PROJECTS
SHOWCASING ALTERNATIVE LIVING & CREATIVE PROJECTS

About creating a website

> **Keywords**
>
> the first thing, nice-looking, within two days

2. INVENTORY

About having a shop on their website

> **Keywords**
>
> the perfect place, sell prints, a fantastic way

Discussion

Q: *What kind of photos do you have stored on your phone or computer? What photos do you think others might be interested in buying? Discuss your ideas with your partner.*

Your ideas	Your partner's ideas

106

Grammar

Noun Phrases Postmodified by *To-Infinitives*

To-infinitives can be used to add some more information to noun phrases. There are primarily three types of *to-infinitive* phrases.

1. Taking the preceding noun as the object.
   There are **many things to do** if you want to maintain a healthy lifestyle.
2. Indicating the content of the preceding noun.
   For many jobs, having **the ability to speak English** is a valuable and often-required skill.
3. Being appositive with the preceding noun.
   The company has **a policy to promote diversity**.

Grammar Exercise

Unscramble the following words and complete the sentences.

1. As an artist, I have a dream (inspires / create / masterpiece / a / that / to / people).

   _____

2. My daughter received (to / and / an opportunity / study / abroad / expand) her horizons.

   _____

3. The need (a global priority / issues / become / address / environmental / has / to).

   _____

4. In our team meeting, each member was (complete / task / assigned / a / to / specific).

   _____

5. (to / was / the office space / the plan / well-received / renovate) by the entire staff.

   _____

6. Students should set (during / to / specific goals / achieve / the first semester / some).

   _____

107

🎵 2-25

The way people work has become more diverse in recent years. More individuals are choosing to work remotely instead of going to the office. However, the benefits of working from the office are also being recognized again. This leads to the question of whether working from home will continue to grow in popularity. To discuss this, we need to consider the advantages and
5 disadvantages from the perspectives of employees, management, and society as a whole.

From the employees' point of view, working from home has the advantage of saving time on commuting. This allows for better time management and more personal time for family and hobbies. Additionally, it eliminates the stress of dealing with heavy traffic and long commutes. On the downside, communication becomes more challenging as there are fewer opportunities for
10 direct interaction and collaboration with colleagues. It can also blur the line between work and personal life, leading to work-related pressures affecting one's private life.

From a management perspective, one major benefit is saving the cost of renting office space. Renting in central areas can be expensive, so working remotely can be a cost-saving opportunity. It also opens up the possibility of hiring talented individuals regardless of their location.
15 However, management faces similar communication difficulties to employees. Ensuring smooth communication and information sharing becomes a challenge. Monitoring work performance and effectively managing remote workers can also be difficult.

Considering society as a whole, telecommuting has the potential to reduce traffic problems, resulting in fewer traffic jams and crowded public transportation. It can also contribute to decreasing
20 carbon dioxide emissions and energy consumption, positively impacting the environment. However, one negative aspect is the widening of the digital divide. Not everyone has equal access to the internet and computers, and telecommuting may make this gap more serious.

In summary, telecommuting has its pros and cons. Different work styles also come with their advantages and disadvantages. As society becomes more diverse, we can expect a variety of
25 working styles to emerge. Practically, we may be entering an era where both companies and society need to accept flexible work lifestyles to sustain themselves.

Vocabulary Check

Fill in the blanks with the words given in the box. Change the word form if necessary.

1. Last night, the raindrops on the window _____ the view of the street outside.
2. Due to the pandemic, many employees were required to _____ and do remote work.
3. The museum's collection is incredibly _____.
4. I looked up and saw that the sun had just _____ from the clouds.
5. The new software program is designed to _____ errors.

| diverse | eliminate | blur | telecommute | emerge |

Reading Comprehension

Answer the following questions.

1. From an employee's perspective, what are the advantages of working from home?

   _____

2. How does working from home impact communication for employees?

   _____

3. From a manager's perspective, what are the disadvantages of working from home?

   _____

4. What are the potential societal benefits of telecommuting?

   _____

UNIT 1 UNIT 2 UNIT 3 UNIT 4 UNIT 5 UNIT 6 UNIT 7 UNIT 8 UNIT 9 UNIT 10 UNIT 11 UNIT 12 UNIT 13 UNIT 14 UNIT 15

Writing

A *Write about your opinions on how people should work in 70-80 words, considering the following points.*

❑ If you were in charge of a company, would you recommend telecommuting or coming to the office?

❑ Are there any disadvantages to this way of working?

❑ How would you overcome them?

B *Make pairs and share your ideas with your partner. Write down what your partner has shared with you.*

Keeping It Local

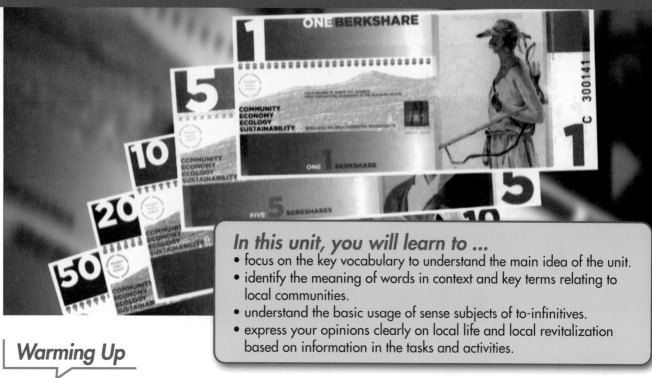

In this unit, you will learn to ...

- focus on the key vocabulary to understand the main idea of the unit.
- identify the meaning of words in context and key terms relating to local communities.
- understand the basic usage of sense subjects of to-infinitives.
- express your opinions clearly on local life and local revitalization based on information in the tasks and activities.

Warming Up

Choose or write your own answers to the following questions. Then ask your partner the questions.

1. By what means do you usually make payments?
   - ❏ Cash
   - ❏ Credit card
   - ❏ Electronic money
   - ❏ Other (   )

2. If you were to create a currency for your local community, what would you print on the front?
   - ❏ Local celebrities
   - ❏ Local products or specialties
   - ❏ Fictional characters associated with the local community
   - ❏ Other (   )

3. Is there a famous person from your local area? If so, what makes that person famous?

_____

Watching WEB動画 🖥 📀DVD 📀CD 2-26

Watch the video and write a brief outline in approximately five sentences.

Vocabulary

A *Choose the most appropriate word from the box to complete the phrases. Change the word form if necessary.*

1. • foreign _____ exchange rates
   • the dollar as a global _____
   • buy a virtual _____

2. • a fashion _____
   • a local _____
   • a popular _____ of organic products

3. • _____ a new laptop
   • the process of _____ a car
   • _____ a new camera from the local store

4. • be _____ a visit
   • be _____ the expensive price
   • be _____ waiting in line

5. • _____ one's savings in the stock market
   • _____ in a startup company
   • _____ in real estate for long-term returns

| currency   worth   retailer   purchase   invest |

B *Choose the most appropriate meaning of the underlined expressions.*

1. A large number of cars were stuck in traffic during rush hour.
   a. Only a few
   b. A lot of
   c. Precious
   d. Very big

2. We decided to expand our business and open chain stores in different cities.
   a. special shops that sell metal strings
   b. independent shops operating in the same area
   c. individual shops specializing in different products
   d. similar shops owned by the same company

Listening Comprehension

A *Watch the video and choose the correct answers to the following questions.*

1. Who is mentioned as an example of local celebrities that appear on printed bills?
   a. Moby Dick
   b. Herman Melville
   c. Abraham Lincoln
   d. Alice Maggio

2. What is Phyllis Webb's occupation in the video?
   a. Local merchant
   b. Economist
   c. Mayor
   d. Banker

3. How many countries around the world have local currencies?

   a. Nearly 13 countries

   b. Nearly 30 countries

   c. Nearly 113 countries

   d. Nearly 130 countries

B *Answer the following questions.*

1. How does using local currency take your relationship a step further with local vendors?

   _____

2. Why does Alice think a large number of communities are going to start local currencies?

   _____

Tips on Listening and Speaking   2-28

Pronouncing Numbers with *-teen* or *-ty*

It can be difficult for non-native speakers to distinguish between the pronunciation of numbers ending in *-teen*, such as 13 and 14, and numbers ending in *-ty*, such as 30 and 40. Numbers ending in *-teen* have the accent on the final syllable (e.g., *fif-TEEN*), whereas numbers ending in *-ty* have the accent at the beginning of the word (e.g., *TWEN-ty*).

I was going to bake <u>50</u> cookies, but I only baked <u>15</u> because I didn't have enough ingredients.   [ˈfɪfti]   [fɪfˈtiːn]

Dictation   2-29

Listen to the sentences and fill in the blanks.

1. With a locally owned business, _____, in your local community.

2. _____, using local vendors.

3. It's about hiring locally, investing locally, and _____.

Retelling

WEB動画　DVD

Watch the video again and tell the story of each scene to your partner. You can use the keywords given next to each picture.

e.g.

About images on BerkShares

(Keywords)

local heroes,　the Berkshire hills, the landscape

Model

On the front side of BerkShares, you can see local heroes. The image of local artwork is on the back. The Berkshire hills are also illustrated on the front side. So, this local currency is a representation of where the local people live and what the landscape is like.

1.

The benefits of adopting local currencies

(Keywords)

cycle,　re-spend,　back into the community

2.

What statistics show

(Keywords)

using a local currency, using a national currency, another part of the country.

Discussion

Q: *Are there any risks associated with creating and using a local currency? Discuss your ideas with your partner.*

Your ideas	Your partner's ideas

Grammar

Sense Subjects of *To-Infinitives*

When the sense subject of a *to-infinitive* does not match the subject of the sentence, the sense subject of a *to-infinitive* can be clarified by inserting the form "for…" before the *to-infinitive*. However, when the *to-infinitive* is used with an adjective describing the characteristics or abilities of a person, such as "kind" or "smart", it is inserted in the form of "of…".

1. The company provided resources <u>for employees</u> to enhance their skills.

        "employees" is the subject of "enhance"

2. It is essential <u>for students</u> to attend class regularly.

    "students" is the subject of "attend"

3. It is considerate <u>of her</u> to give up her seat for the elderly.

    "her" is the subject of "give up"

Grammar Exercise

Unscramble the following words and complete the sentences.

1. It's necessary (be / us / to / for / of / aware) the risks involved.

_____

2. (the company / generous / to / it's / donate / of) a portion of their profits to charity.

_____

3. The coach designed a training program (to / for / improve / their / athletes / performance).

_____

4. It's wise (for / money / you / save / of / to) the future.

_____

5. The organization offers scholarships (students / pursue / higher / to / education / for).

_____

6. It was careless (me / of / at home / to / my wallet / have left).

_____

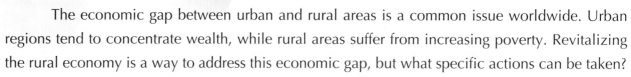

🎵 2-30

The economic gap between urban and rural areas is a common issue worldwide. Urban regions tend to concentrate wealth, while rural areas suffer from increasing poverty. Revitalizing the rural economy is a way to address this economic gap, but what specific actions can be taken?

Now, let's explore some local revitalization endeavors undertaken by Japanese university
5 students and institutions. First, we have a case study of a student from Kanagawa Prefecture who embarked on a research project. In Saga Prefecture, she organized a workshop in collaboration with local residents to boost the area's appeal following a decline in tourism. Additionally, she worked in Saitama Prefecture, establishing a cafeteria at a local gathering place to foster interaction between generations, particularly between the elderly and children. She aims to promote exchange
10 between generations through food-based activities like using local vegetables in curry or having fish barbecues.

Furthermore, an increasing number of universities are implementing regional training programs. For instance, one university in Tokyo offers a 150-day regional training program, enabling students to choose from a wide range of suggested regions to stay. During their stay,
15 students immerse themselves in the community, collaborating with local residents not only to organize events and support local industries but also to explore solutions for various community issues. Such long-term student involvement is expected to yield positive economic effects in the area.

Lastly, we highlight the efforts of some students from Wakayama Prefecture. They are
20 operating a café in a vacant space within a deserted shopping arcade, which faced challenges due to aging store owners and management issues. This project won first prize in a business competition, and the students have become confident that this has become a viable ongoing activity. These local revitalization activities allow students to enhance their planning and implementation skills. The activities benefit not only the economic and community development of the area but also the
25 students' personal growth.

Revitalizing the local economy is crucial for sustainable development and prosperity of a region. It leads to job creation, growth of local businesses, and an enhanced quality of life for the local residents. If you could embark on a challenge for local revitalization, what would you like to do?

Vocabulary Check

Fill in the blanks with the words given in the box. Change the word form if necessary.

1. The company's investment in employee training _____ higher productivity and improved job satisfaction during the preceding fiscal year.

2. Last year, Emma _____ on a journey to explore different cultures and countries around the world.

3. The city's economic decline led to many businesses closing down, leaving behind _____ office buildings and factories.

4. The community center is hosting skill-building programs to _____ the local workforce and provide new employment opportunities.

5. The virtual reality game is designed to _____ players in a realistic and interactive world.

revitalize   embark   immerse   yield   deserted

Reading Comprehension

Answer the following questions.

1. How does the student from Kanagawa Prefecture promote interaction between generations in Saitama Prefecture?

   _____

2. What type of programs are universities implementing to support local revitalization?

   _____

3. Why have the students from Wakayama prefecture become confident?

   _____

4. What are the benefits of revitalizing the local economy mentioned in the passage?

   _____

Writing

A *Propose a project for local revitalization, and write about it in 70-80 words, considering the following points.*

❑ If you participate in an activity for local revitalization, what type of activity would you engage in?

❑ What are the potential barriers to achieving the goals of the activity?

❑ What would you do to overcome those barriers?

B *Make pairs and share your ideas with your partner. Write down what your partner has shared with you.*

The Mystery of the Axe

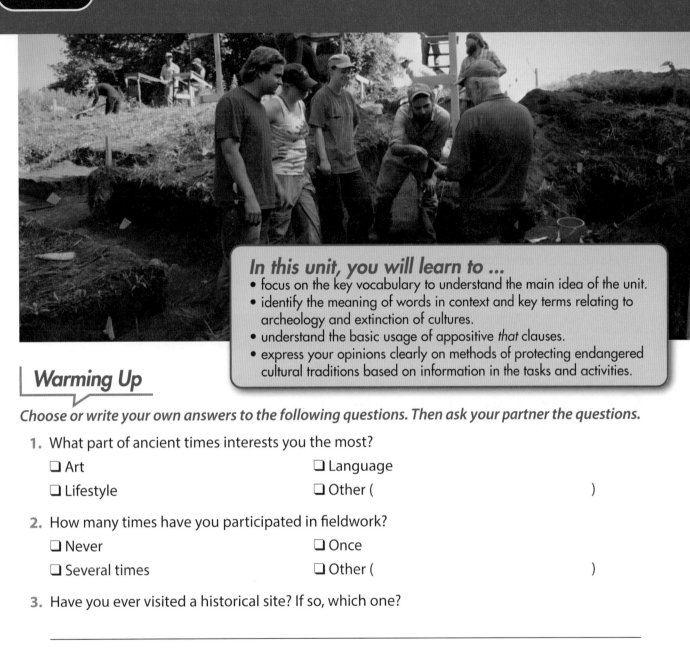

In this unit, you will learn to ...
- focus on the key vocabulary to understand the main idea of the unit.
- identify the meaning of words in context and key terms relating to archeology and extinction of cultures.
- understand the basic usage of appositive *that* clauses.
- express your opinions clearly on methods of protecting endangered cultural traditions based on information in the tasks and activities.

Warming Up

Choose or write your own answers to the following questions. Then ask your partner the questions.

1. What part of ancient times interests you the most?
   - ❏ Art
   - ❏ Lifestyle
   - ❏ Language
   - ❏ Other (   )

2. How many times have you participated in fieldwork?
   - ❏ Never
   - ❏ Several times
   - ❏ Once
   - ❏ Other (   )

3. Have you ever visited a historical site? If so, which one?

_____

Watching

WEB動画 DVD CD 2-31

Watch the video and write a brief outline in approximately five sentences.

Vocabulary 🔊 2-32

A *Choose the most appropriate word from the box to complete the phrases. Change the word form if necessary.*

1. • an important _____ in solving the mystery
   • footprints serving as a _____
   • a message containing several _____

2. • _____ tattoos on the suspect's arm
   • the _____ symbol of the company's logo
   • the _____ quality making it different

3. • a colonial _____
   • a _____ where Native Americans live
   • land for a _____

4. • preserve an ancient _____
   • discover a rare _____ like a ceramic vase
   • uncover a medieval _____

5. • _____ breakthroughs made by the scientist
   • the _____ view from the mountaintop
   • _____ tricks performed by the magician

artifact   settlement   clue   astonishing   distinctive

B *Choose the most appropriate meaning of the underlined expressions.*

1. The <u>archeological</u> site in Greece is a UNESCO World Heritage Site.
   a. primitive
   b. artistic
   c. literary
   d. historical

2. I can say <u>for sure</u> that it's going to rain today, based on the dark clouds and thunder.
   a. certainly
   b. randomly
   c. perhaps
   d. doubtfully

Listening Comprehension WEB動画 DVD CD 2-31

A *Watch the video and choose the correct answers to the following questions.*

1. What type of iron tool does Ron think the object was?
   a. A blade
   b. A sword
   c. A planing tool
   d. An axe

2. What did the special mark on the axe resemble?
   a. A reversed "g"
   b. A sideways "b"
   c. A reversed "2"
   d. A sideways "#"

3. Where did Andrea go to confirm if the mark on the axe matched the one she found?

   a. North America

   b. Latin America

   c. Europe

   d. Asia

B *Answer the following questions.*

1. What kind of facility did Ron and Andrea go to find clues about the origin of the iron tool?

   _____

2. What question does the discovery of the iron axe raise about its journey?

   _____

Tips on Listening and Speaking 2-33

Difference in Pronunciation between "Can" and "Can't"

It is not easy to distinguish between "can" and "can't" since the "t" in "can't" is not pronounced clearly. The difference in pronunciation between "can" and "can't" is that "can" is pronounced with a short vowel sound (/kən/) while "can't" is pronounced with a long vowel sound.

   1. "I **can** speak Spanish." - The word "can" is pronounced with a short vowel sound.
   2. "I **can't** speak Spanish." - The word "can't" is pronounced with a long vowel sound.

Dictation 2-34

Listen to the sentences and fill in the blanks.

1. When I arrived there, I don't think _____ .

2. George, you know, _____ .

3. _____

   means that it's probably not imagination.

Retelling

WEB動画 📺📼 💿 DVD

Watch the video again and tell the story of each scene to your partner. You can use the keywords given next to each picture.

e.g.

The place where an archaeological object is found

> **Keywords**
> a Huron Indian settlement,
> Native American history,
> an Indiana Jones moment

Model

An object is found at the archeological site of a Huron Indian settlement in Canada. This is such a huge discovery that it could change our understanding of Native American history. This is like an Indiana Jones moment.

1.

What Ron learns about the iron axe

> **Keywords**
> made in Europe,   significant,
> the earliest European piece

2.

Further research by Andrea

> **Keywords**
> a private collection of artifacts,
> a meat cleaver,
> on the screen

Discussion

Q: *What do you think is the significance of archeological research? Discuss your ideas with your partner.*

Your ideas	Your partner's ideas

Grammar

Appositive *That* Clause

An appositive *that* clause is a grammatical structure that involves placing a clause after a noun. It renames or explains the preceding noun, providing additional information about that noun.

The notion **that time heals all wounds** is often considered true.

Other examples of nouns that can precede an appositive *that* clause:
argument, belief, claim, decision, fact, hope, hypothesis, idea, news, possibility, report, request, rumor, suggestion, theory

Grammar Exercise

Unscramble the following words and complete the sentences.

1. Researchers were puzzled by (yielded / the fact / unexpected / that / results / the experiment).

   _____

2. (that / a better day / be / the hope / tomorrow / will) than today keeps us going.

   _____

3. Health experts support (exercise / overall / boosts / well-being / the claim / that / regular).

   _____

4. (that / improves / the method / efficiency / the hypothesis / energy) has been verified by many studies.

   _____

5. (we / approach / the suggestion / should / adopt / a / more sustainable / that) has gained support from a lot of people.

   _____

6. We discussed (the event / be / that / might / canceled / the possibility) due to weather.

   _____

CD 2-35

The Hurons are one of the indigenous peoples of North America. They have traditionally spoken the Wyandot language of the Iroquois language group. Wyandot is classified by UNESCO as a language in danger of extinction. It is a worldwide phenomenon that many languages spoken by indigenous peoples, including Wyandot, are in danger of extinction. For example, the language
5 of the Ainu people in the Hokkaido region of Japan is a language in danger of extinction. UNESCO has proclaimed the period 2022-32 as the "International Decade of Indigenous Languages" to help promote and protect indigenous languages and improve the lives of those who speak and sign them.

Now, let us return to the Hurons. Until the 15th century, they lived on the northern shore
10 of what is now Lake Ontario before they were exposed to other cultures. Then in 1615, they first met the French explorer Samuel de Champlain. At that time, they called themselves "Wyandot." By that, they meant "inhabitants of the peninsula" or "islanders." The early French explorers named them Hurons.

Prior to the arrival of the French, the Hurons were in conflict with
15 the Iroquois Confederacy to the south. By the late 16th century, several thousand Hurons lived in central West Virginia. However, forced out by the Iroquois Confederacy, they invaded what is now New York State in the 17th century to secure hunting grounds for the beaver fur trade. Once the Europeans became involved in the fur trade, conflicts between the tribes

Samuel de Champlain

20 to control the trade became quite severe. The French made an alliance with the Hurons, who were the most advanced traders of their time. On the other hand, the Iroquois Confederacy tended to make alliances with the Dutch and English.

In the video of this unit, it was indicated that the origin of the object that was discovered in the Huron settlement may have been the Basque Country. The Basque Country refers to the
25 historical homeland of the Basque people and the Basque language. The region is located at the foothills of the Pyrenees Mountains and bordered by both France and Spain. Considering the Huron people's connection to Europe and the location of the Basque Country, the axe mystery discovered by Ron's research group might be solved.

Vocabulary Check

Fill in the blanks with the words given in the box. Change the word form if necessary.

1. The city's population has grown rapidly, attracting new _____ from all over the country.
2. The Southern states formed the _____ during the American Civil War.
3. The government has taken steps to protect the rights and land of _____ peoples.
4. The _____ between the labor union and environmental groups aims to promote sustainable practices in the workplace.
5. The hunting of elephants has brought them closer to _____.

> indigenous   extinction   inhabitant   alliance   confederacy

Reading Comprehension

Answer the following questions.

1. According to the passage, which language is in danger of extinction in the Hokkaido region of Japan?

   _____

2. What is the purpose of the "International Decade of Indigenous Languages" proclaimed by UNESCO?

   _____

3. What did the Hurons use to call themselves when they first encountered Samuel de Champlain?

   _____

4. Which European power made an alliance with the Hurons?

   _____

125

Writing

A *Write about some ideas you have on measures to protect languages in danger of extinction in 70-80 words, considering the following points.*

❏ What do you think are the reasons for UNESCO to protect endangered languages?

❏ What methods of international cooperation should be employed for such protection?

❏ How can schools increase awareness of such protection activities?

B *Make pairs and share your ideas with your partner. Write down what your partner has shared with you.*

Appendix

Useful Expressions for Discussions

Reacting

- ☐ I see your point.
- ☐ I find that quite interesting [amazing / outstanding / intriguing].
- ☐ That's a good [great / key / fundamental] idea.
- ☐ Really? I didn't know [wasn't aware of] that.
- ☐ Could you please elaborate?
- ☐ I'm intrigued. Tell me more.

Giving your opinion

- ☐ In my opinion [In my view / From my perspective], …
- ☐ I think [believe / feel / suppose] …
- ☐ My opinion [idea / stance / belief] is that …
- ☐ I'd like to say [express] that …
- ☐ As far as I can see, …

Giving yourself time to think

- ☐ Let me take a moment to think.
- ☐ That's an interesting question that requires some thought.
- ☐ I've never considered that before.

Asking for clarification

- ☐ Could you kindly repeat that?
- ☐ Would you mind speaking a bit slower?
- ☐ Could you rephrase that, please?
- ☐ Can you simplify your explanation?
- ☐ Could you clarify what you meant by …

Agreeing

- [ ] I totally [entirely / completely / strongly] agree with you.
- [ ] I agree with your idea [opinion / thought / suggestion / proposal].
- [ ] I'm in complete agreement.
- [ ] I see no objections to that.
- [ ] That certainly makes sense to me.
- [ ] I'm with you on this.

Disagreeing politely

- [ ] I appreciate your point, but I think …
- [ ] I understand your perspective, but in my view, …
- [ ] It's an interesting viewpoint, but I have a different perspective.
- [ ] While that may be true, I would argue that …

Showing importance

- [ ] A is important [crucial / significant / essential], because …
- [ ] One crucial factor to consider is …
- [ ] The key focus here is …
- [ ] We must prioritize [put priority on] … because …

Focusing on one topic

- [ ] On this particular issue [matter / topic / aspect / case / point], …
- [ ] When it comes to this specific point, …
- [ ] Regarding this matter, …

Useful Expressions for Discussions

Explaining in more detail

- [ ] Allow me to expand on this.
- [ ] What I'm trying to convey is that …

Describing the pros

- [ ] One advantage [benefit / merit / strength] is that …
- [ ] One of the positive [good / strong / beneficial] points of A may be that …
- [ ] Another positive feature is …

Describing the cons

- [ ] One disadvantage [drawback / demerit / weakness] is that …
- [ ] The disadvantages include …
- [ ] Another drawback is …

Adding ideas

- [ ] In addition, we could consider …
- [ ] Furthermore, it might be worthwhile to think about …
- [ ] An additional idea to consider is …
- [ ] Another aspect to explore is …
- [ ] One more thing to take into account is …

Checking the other person's understanding

- [ ] Do you understand what I mean?
- [ ] Do you follow me?
- [ ] Are you with me?
- [ ] Do you know what I mean?

Checking your own understanding

☐ So, you're saying that …?

☐ If I understand correctly, you believe that …?

☐ Your viewpoint is that …, is that right?

Referring to a source

☐ As the newspaper reports [says / shows / indicates], …

☐ The study revealed [found / discovered / demonstrated] that …

☐ According to an article I read [encountered / reviewed / summarized / came across], …

☐ The data indicates [suggests / implies / illustrates] that …

☐ As the article emphasizes [highlights / underscores], …

Not sure

☐ I'm not sure.

☐ I suppose [guess] so.

☐ I don't have a clear answer.

☐ It's difficult to give a complete answer.

Web動画のご案内　**StreamLine**

本テキストの映像は、オンラインでのストリーミング再生になります。下記URLよりご利用ください。なお**有効期限は、はじめてログインした時点から1年半**です。

http://st.seibido.co.jp

1 ログイン画面

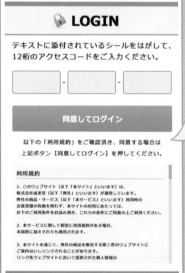

巻末に添付されているシールをはがして、アクセスコードをご入力ください。

2 メニュー画面

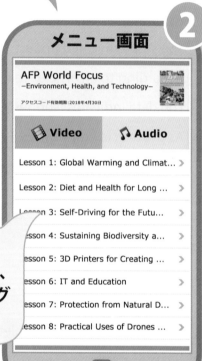

「Video」または「Audio」を選択すると、それぞれストリーミング再生ができます。

3 再生画面

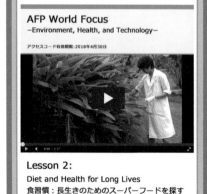

推奨動作環境

【PC OS】
Windows 7～ ／ Mac 10.8～

【Mobile OS】
iOS ／ Android ※Androidの場合は4.x～が推奨

【Desktop ブラウザ】
Internet Explorer 9～ / Firefox / Chrome / Safari

Global Gate TESTUDY のご案内

STUDY 学習内容

教科書の学習をWeb上に再現しております。
リアルタイムで学習状況を確認することができます。

教科書タスク	TESTUDY 学習形式
Warming Up	多肢選択問題
Watching	動画再生
Vocabulary	タイピング問題
Listening Comprehension	動画再生および多肢選択問題など
Dictation	タイピング問題
Retelling	動画再生および自由記入フォーム
Discussion	自由記入フォーム
Grammar Exercise	語句整序問題
Reading	本文掲載
Vocabulary Check	タイピング問題
Reading Comprehension	自由記入フォーム
Writing	自由記入フォーム

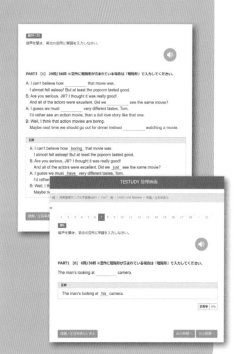

REVIEW 学習内容

授業の復習に活用することができます。

教科書タスク	TESTUDY 学習形式
Vocabulary	多肢選択問題
Tips on Listening and Speaking	音声認識学習
Dictation	タイピング問題
Grammar Exercise	語句整序問題

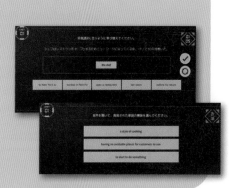

著者

田中 広宣	（東京医療保健大学 非常勤講師）
五十嵐 美加	（青山学院大学 非常勤講師）
Bill Benfield	（株式会社成美堂）
森田 彰	（早稲田大学 教授）

TEXT PRODUCTION STAFF

edited by	編集
Takashi Kudo	工藤 隆志
Eiichi Tamura	田村 栄一
Mitsugu Shishido	宍戸 貢
Hiroshi Yoshizuka	吉塚 弘
cover design by	表紙デザイン
Nobuyoshi Fujino	藤野 伸芳
DTP by	DTP
ALIUS (Hiroyuki Kinouchi)	アリウス（木野内 宏行）

CD PRODUCTION STAFF

recorded by	吹き込み者
Dominic Allen (AmE)	ドミニク・アレン（アメリカ英語）
Howard Colefield (AmE)	ハワード・コールフィルド（アメリカ英語）
Rachel Walzer (AmE)	レイチェル・ワルザー（アメリカ英語）
Karen Headrich (AmE)	カレン・ヘドリック（アメリカ英語）

Global Gate Upper-intermediate
-Video-based Four Skills Training-

2024年1月20日　初版発行
2024年2月15日　第2刷発行

著　者	田中 広宣　五十嵐 美加
	Bill Benfield　森田 彰
発 行 者	佐野 英一郎
発 行 所	株式会社 成美堂
	〒101-0052　東京都千代田区神田小川町3-22
	TEL 03-3291-2261　FAX 03-3293-5490
	https://www.seibido.co.jp

印 刷・製 本　三美印刷株式会社

ISBN 978-4-7919-7283-8　　　　　　　　　　　　Printed in Japan